AMAZON FBA

A Step by Step Beginner's Guide To Selling on
Amazon, Making Money, Be an Amazon
Seller, Launch Private Label Products, and
Earn Passive Income From Your Online Business

JAMES MOORE

Introduction

Hi, I'm James Moore. Thanks so much for joining me here today. I'm going to share some intrinsic knowledge with you with regard to Amazon FBA (fulfilment by Amazon). It's my distinct aim that you get a wealth of information from this title, because that's my number one goal here. So let's make a start together. You'll have a good understanding in no time.

Entrepreneurs around the globe are offered (by Amazon) the world's largest platform for e-commerce projects. This is great news! As you would already know, it has a database full of customers, and it's easy to see why so many "on the ball" business owners have undertaken dropshipping as a means to establish a viable business alternative to their daily 9-5 grind.

It might sound easy to perform. However, this doesn't mean that anyone who attempts selling on Amazon *will* become successful. There is a steep learning curve involved, and many variables you need to consider.

In this comprehensive guide, I'll aim to take the novice, or the entrepreneur who is making their first steps on their journey toward success, forward. And I'll begin to formulate and validate any product idea in mind, and also to help navigate you through the steps needed to design your product, including how to locate a host of valuable suppliers.

E-commerce is a billion-dollar industry, and there are still markets yet to be tapped into which are ripe for exploitation and where you may make a healthy profit. Further in the guide, we'll explore the terminology and the nuances which are vital in effective communication (and for building successful relationships with your suppliers).

I'll take you through finding that very first product, and the chance to go further and create your own brand. And as you'll see, it isn't as easy as merely sourcing a product and selling it. In fact, a product must serve a particular market and have that little bit of "something special" which sets you apart from any competition. This, in turn, gives customers a reason to choose your product and brand above anyone else.

Once you have listed products, that is only part of the job, we'll also guide you through listings which prove useful (including the all-important successful launch and marketing campaigns) which help generate substantial returns on investment.

This comprehensive guide covers all you need to know to enter one of the most significant opportunities which exists on the web, and which provides you the opportunity to work with one of the largest and fastest growing companies in the world. Amazon!!!

Strategies for a Good Idea, and What Makes One

CHAPTER 1

Every entrepreneur asks the same question at the beginning of their road toward working with Amazon.

"What is the one awesome thing I should sell?"

Although this is the first step, it is a crucial one in the process because it sets in motion each of the tasks after it that will be performed. If an entrepreneur only has a generic idea which is uninspired and merely following the crowd, you'll find it much harder the successfully complete all of the steps which follow and lead you toward a business which is profitable.

Anyone who follows ideas which are classed as a general "crowd following" exercise will never attain a profitable business plan. When this happens, all that occurs (in most cases) is that an entrepreneur carries on where others have been, and where the other party, at that point, have already made their profit. Having your own idea of emerging trends can have you placed at the head of the game, and then it is up to others to follow you! This is the right mindset needed here.

Any niche which is seen as profitable becomes saturated with supply, which then quickly leads to oversupply. Profits can be driven down as prices drop, and the entire process becomes much harder to control.

A budding entrepreneur must come up with the solution, and to come up with ideas in niche areas which are still untapped, including having the potential to meet customer demand. Any ideas must be well-validated to make sure it is a suitable candidate before following on with the following steps. To do this, we'll follow a checklist for each idea and determine if it will be profitable or not. You might have noticed we are talking about multiples, and this is done for good reason. You should never only focus on one item, mostly because an attachment to that product creeps in.

With paper and a pen, we can take the first step of going over our ideas and validating them, and see if they are worthy of pursuing. Although, you don't want too much attachment to the products you sell, you do need some interest, though, as this can affect your performance later. If you've got no passion for your products, you're less likely to have that extra bit of a push to see it through until the end. Ultimately, this would affect the majority of your profit. You should also not pursue ideas because you feel they can generate a lot of money. There are bound to be times when you have yet to reach a profitable stage, and as you have no care for the product, you might quit. You don't want to do this before you see a return and hit the "gold mine," so to speak.

Profitable Products and Three Strategies to Find Them

We can take a look at three key strategies to determine if your ideas will be worthy of pursuing and going on to be profitable products. It might be the case that one approach appears to be sufficient, but, I advise on completing all three before proceeding further toward validating your ideas. Each strategy will reveal demand for your potential ideas and will allow you to fully understand if there is a need for these products, and if customers are, in fact, searching for them.

Amazon's Engine

Amazon itself can be used to undertake the first strategy where you can find which products are currently selling successfully. Once you begin typing in the search bar, as little as one letter will provide you with a drop-down list of suggested products. And, being able to see what people are searching for, you can determine the strength of demand for your product, so you'll quickly see if your ideas have any value.

As a good example, if you were searching for cat products, you'll see numerous suggestions which are preceded by the word "cat." These could include "cat litter," "cat trees," "cat scratching post," among many others. From this list, you can receive a nice list of ideas in areas which are worthy of exploring for products under the term "cat." It also presents you with what people are searching for in products which are related to cats. By doing this vital step, it goes to prove that there *is* a demand for these products.

For inspiration, you can quickly go through each letter of the alphabet, and you'll see the products which are the hottest being displayed which begin with each letter. Once you have done this, you can merely add a second letter and go through searching again to find ideas you can add to, just for your personal brainstorming list. I like doing this; I find it super fun, actually. You might be shocked at some of them.

It should be noted, some of these items are already being sold in mass volume, so be careful not to choose something already being sold in massive quantities in a saturated niche. Some more checking is required here.

A second way to use Amazon to your overall advantage is: by navigating through and checking the other items which customers have been viewing as an addition to the main item. This gives a much greater insight into the chosen niche which you are researching and, at the same time, you might spot fun and exciting products which spark some interest. This can work really well if you are only looking at categories alone, mostly because Amazon contains many categories which you can search quickly. This will be explained further (and later) in the title.

As with the previous method, you can view what customers have already purchased using Amazon's search engine, and what they are considering buying. This can provide a good idea of how a niche performs and how customers make their purchases by going between the different types of items.

Using these methods might not present whether or not these ideas are making a profit, but it is an unlimited source of ideas which are new to you. If and when you find yourself struggling to come up with something which is new, or your first list tends to fall toward generic items which can be purchased in many other areas, it's a great method. Actually, ideas which are unique, and products that are sought after and in high demand will be found using this strategy. Just make sure your product (as in the *exact* same one) isn't on there already, a hundred gazillion times, because then the competition will be too great for any real profit to be had.

Sometimes, a good many ideas come from looking around the home. However, this won't result in many items which would go on to make a successful Amazon business. When you use the power of Amazon's search engine, you can efficiently collect information which you can add to your brainstorming list, even if you just build it to peruse later on.

Having a Golden Touch

If you find you wish to take longer in researching product ideas, and sitting at a computer for extended periods hinders your creative thinking, this method could help stir your creative juices... and is a method you can use during a regular day.

It's a straightforward method and involves writing down everything you touched in the previous hour. It might appear to be an enormous undertaking, but it highlights items which you take for granted and might overlook as something which is worth pursuing.

It is best to try this technique when you are out of ideas and want to get your mind working in ways where conventional thinking isn't helping much. This method can also help you gather ideas in an accelerated way, as the number of items you touch can be staggering. An example being: when you wake up. You can find that you touch your pillow, your bedsheets, alarm clock, and slippers. Instantly you've got four items which can give further ideas. You can already see this technique is useful, and, as time goes on, you'll see more and more items that you touch and use which could be worth further exploration.

What you should note is: these are not items you're looking to sell, because these are stems of ideas for further exploration where you can go deeper and see the function of these items while they are in your hands. Over the course of a week (with which you should perform this task) you'll see many items which would never cross your mind throughout the day. Once you're in the habit of writing them down, you'll see that inspiration begins flowing, and ideas for products which can bring a benefit to customers will become second nature.

The thinking behind this technique is that: as you're a consumer, you obtain a greater understanding of the product and how it can be improved, or how it is able to add benefit to customers. Bearing this in mind, you can easily branch out with your final ideas in new ways, so the products you've listed will deliver that value more sufficiently.

Bricks and Mortar Retail

The final method requires you to do some offline research. Before there was e-commerce, this method was what the first pioneers did to give them ideas of what to sell online. What you need to do is visit a large store and see what is stocked on their shelves. If you scour each of their departments (such as electrical, toys, and home-wares) you can note down the items which are located in key positions, this is an indication of which products are the better sellers.

You might also find many of these products are already selling well on Amazon. However, there is always the chance to find that "hidden gem" which hasn't yet reached being exposed online, and you can take advantage of key products like this for your business.

Later, we'll explore more marketing techniques which you can use when you are checking in the bricks and mortar stores.

Benefits of Jungle Scout

All of the above methods are free, yet there is one which is far better than these and, for this reason, there is a monthly fee. It does offer much higher value when you want to take your business to the next level, and the investment is well worth it, in my opinion.

Jungle Scout works by allowing you to view Amazon's database in full, and making good use of filters which you use to fine-tune your search. Amazon has over 20 million products in its database which increases each day, and when you make full use of these filters, you can hone in on niches which are untapped and fully exploit that high-demand product.

The main advantage of Jungle Scout is it only lists products which are, in fact, selling. This makes it useful (compared to a list of products which aren't selling). Now you can see products which are bringing the most profit, and you can sort by market, price, customer reviews, and the quality of the product listing, which is key by the way.

When you search for underperforming listings which contain very profitable products, you can see areas where the market is letting good customers down. You can then take this and use it to gain an advantage against these underperforming competitors.

At the same time, you'll need to read reviews as you will gain an insight into the quality of each product, and any products not being reviewed in a favorable light. There are customers there for those products, but they are not satisfied with the current suppliers. *Why?* This is a golden opportunity for you.

Jungle Scout comes in two forms, and the first being a desktop app, it can also be installed as a chrome extension for when you are browsing Amazon's website. This provides you with information on all listings you check on. With estimated revenue, numbers of reviews, ratings, prices offered, and the expected sales (among other things) which are of great use. One of the most beneficial pieces of information is if the item is on an upward or downward trend. This highlights if there is still demand, or if it is a product which should be scrubbed (if you have it on your list).

Jungle Scout is a powerful tool and using it means you have all the power of Amazon behind you, and at your disposal. When you start growing your Amazon business, you can fully exploit data provided by this tool, and if you're just getting started with a limited capital, you might find paying for a month or two is sufficient. This way, it avoids you committing to something in which you might need to change your mind on. But, at the end of the day, Jungle Scout takes away all of that guesswork when you want to come up with new ideas.

Ideas and Validating Them

CHAPTER 2

We've explored some simple ways in which you can get those creative juices flowing, and how to generate your potential Amazon product ideas for the next step in the process. Here we'll see if your idea has any value, or if it is better to let others take their chance on them. This will be the final step in accepting your idea for your niche and entering the market.

Assessing ideas offers background research you perform in determining if your ideas do have value.

To do this, there are a number of criterion used in assessing your ideas such as:

- Demand
- Profit
- Passion
- Competition
- Customer Lifetime Value

Product Demand

This is the first criteria, and is one of the most important. Actually, no demand means no customers are searching for the product, and you'll find it nearly impossible to make a profit if this is the case.

The best products to supply are ones which have a high demand, and this is where there are a vast number of people who are searching for the exact same product. If you finally end up providing one of these high demand products which users use in everyday life, you'll quickly see your business becoming successful.

Everything begins with demand, and that's why it is the chief criteria. When you take a look at demand, it can be broken down further into three other criterion, which helps determine the demand for the product. The first demand criteria is revenue, which is earned from your product, and you can decide if any chosen product is in high demand if it's making sales for your competitors.

If sales are being made in the niche, it means there is still a significant profit to be made when selling that specific product. If there happens to be another seller entering into the niche, such as yourself, you should be able to take a piece of the action and a share of the market, unless it's totally swamped.

Uptrend data is the next criteria where specific niches will experience an increase in sales, as well as downward trends in the popularity of a product throughout a year. Some products are hot sales in the early months of the year, only to be sat waiting for buyers over the next few months. An excellent recent example of this is the fidget spinner, and during the middle of 2017, they were immensely popular. Many resellers jumped on the craze to make money from the trend, only to find this craze waned, and so they were left with too much stock which could not be sold.

It shows that many of these resellers might not have focused on the downward trend toward the year's end. Much is the same with seasonal products being stocked. A primary example here, being: items which are popular in the lead up to Christmas, but at other times sales become flat. It's crucial you keep an eye on these trends and see how they react over a period, and you need to consider how long a trend would remain in force.

The next and final criteria can be a way of validating the previous two as a way to determine the overall demand for a product. If you use the 10-4 rule, you can see which products experience strong demand, and for how long this demand stays in place. It is possible (when selling products cheaply) to boost their rankings. However, this would fudge the data and products would not be selling as well if they were to remain at their regular price.

To explain the 10-4 rule goes like this: The four in the rule represents four thousand dollars, and it means two to three products should be making sales of around four thousand dollars per month.

Product Competition

Competition can be seen as the direct antithesis of demand, and when there is high demand for products, there is lots of competition. There is a delicate balance which must be understood before you enter a market. If the balance swings toward a supplier, there will be too much competition for the demand. This is where the market is saturated, and prices become slashed to shift product. As a result, profit margins fall to unhealthy levels.

On the contrary, where there is high demand and little competition, you will find that this is where there is serious money to be made from your products. With this in mind, you need to find the place in your niche where you can work with lower than average competition, and this way, everyone can share the profits within the niche.

You can validate your competition on Amazon by performing a simple rule, and then find if the niche is desirable to enter. What you do is take three by a hundred, three hundred. Let me explain. What this means is you need three products to be on the first page which have less than 100 reviews, and you will also want an average of lower than 300 reviews on the first page.

The reason for this is: you want your product listing to be showing on the first page of Amazon (compared to being a few pages in) after a search has been conducted. As with many things in search, people will use items listed on the first page, and not venture further down the list of results.

When you have products which are competing against ones which have less than 100 reviews, it means you can reach that number in a short time and, in effect, leapfrog your customers and rank higher in the Amazon search. Eventually, this would lead you to receive more sales. You need to be aware though, it is of little use competing with anyone whose product has thousands of reviews, because this is an indication their sales position is too strong, and it would be challenging for you to enter the market with any amount of success.

You can see this in markets which contain sportswear, and the items are branded, and it isn't too hard to understand there is no way you can compete with this at the same price and quality. It is for reasons such as this that you'll need to drill down further into niches, and then you can create a market for products which are not holding any significant players.

This rule is flexible, and how you use it is at your discretion. However, around 300 is the general rule to give a good indication the product you're researching is in high demand, while at the same time not having a significant brand to contend with.

It is unfortunate that the higher the amount of competition, the less profit you can make, but keep in mind, areas which have high profit and little competition typically don't last that long. As you are researching your niche, other resellers are doing the same, so any niches which are wide open and ripe for entering won't last long before competition creeps into them. Keep this in mind.

When you are conducting your research, you should take this as motivation to exploit these areas in as quick a time as is possible, and take full advantage of the profitable areas while they are still there for the taking. You can also differentiate the competition as a means of boosting your potential in taking a much higher percentage of the market share. You can do this through development and innovation of your products, and this; we will go into in much broader detail later in the title.

Product Profit

Profitability is the third part of validating a product and is essential for any Amazon business to continue, and to make sure there is a healthy return on investment. The last thing anyone wants is: to invest a heap of cash and effort in bringing products to market, only to find that they are not as profitable as first hoped. When this happens, the worst case scenario is that there will be a loss, and a best case is you can get back any money you have invested... hopefully.

This is one crucial element which shouldn't be left to chance, so, due diligence and research are essential in this area before you commit to supplying products on Amazon. With this in mind, Amazon has created an official calculator which you can make use of on their website. As it's been designed by them, it is perfectly poised to let you know the exact amount of money you can make from each sale that you create by using Amazon.

To begin, you would open Jungle Scout. For this quick example, we will use dining and kitchen. The price range which we will investigate is $14 to $50, between 1 thru 2500. Here, we will sort by pricing. One of the first things you'll notice will be around half a million per month, and at this stage, you should open up the item listing and check the average price for that specific keyword or for the particular item it relates to.

At this point, you should check a few prices, because it is possible that some prices have been overinflated or they have been underpriced. Once you have hold of this information, insert it into the data section and then head to the wholesale site which you have decided to use. This could be either:

- Alibaba

- Salehoo
- Oberlo

These are examples.

Use these (or any others from which you have chosen), then you will search for the exact same items on these sites, and make sure that the data is an exact match. Once you search for an average price, you might find some products are coming with accessories, so these should be avoided as the information won't be an exact match, and any calculation you make will not be correct.

When you have found the average price of the exact product on these sites, you enter this into Amazon's calculator, and it will return the result of what you stand to make after all fees have been paid. Amazon's calculator will show (in detail) the costs. However, you are able to customize this to fall in line with how you plan on running your business.

Areas you need to consider are:

- Warehousing
- Shipping from your supplier
- Transportation to and from Amazon
- Advertising

Ideally, if you can make a substantial profit straight away, that is best. By using their calculator with all your costs inputted, you can receive an estimate of the net profit you could make with each sale.

As a note, any products under $10 aren't worth selling on Amazon, mostly due to the imposed fees and shipping costs which will quickly eat away at the tiny profit you might make.

When you use the calculator, you will see which of the products offer a potentially high-profit margin, along with ones which are best to leave alone, as they come with a high amount of risk. If you find your overall revenue is three times that of your purchase price, you stand to make a decent amount of profit with your products after all the fees and costs have been taken into account. When you come to examine profit, make sure to consider any other factors you're using when you are attempting to validate your product, as these will play a crucial part in how your products are going to perform.

In addition to all this, you could think that products which have a lower than average profit margin are risky to undertake, however, if you can see there are masses of demand, it could be a product which people are continually looking for. With this in mind, a product of this type could sell more volume than products which have higher profit margins, yet a lower demand.

Note: research plenty of items before you arrive at your final decision, especially when it comes to your profitability. You will have lots that you need to consider. You might come to find a product isn't selling well on Amazon, yet it has high potential so it might have a good reason behind it.

Feed Your Passion

Have you ever noticed some of the world's wealthiest people continue working well into their golden years when they could be enjoying the fruits of their labors? We know they don't need the money, and retirement isn't an issue to them. They do it because they love what they do, and they continue to do so as long as they can, because of their passion.

You'll find that if you do something purely for the money, any passion will quickly wane as there is no pleasure factor in what you are doing, or hoping to achieve. Material gains which take a lot of effort are never enough to satisfy anyone. That's a whole other book, so I'll let you discern your opinion on that topic.

It's often overlooked, but passion is one of the most crucial aspects of creating a successful Amazon business. If you're not enjoying what you're doing, you won't overcome any of the challenges you'll meet head-on. You stand a much higher chance of success if you have a passion for your product, and are possibly a user of it, yourself. This can present new ways in which to improve it, and what you can do when something goes wrong, and this you'll find is really useful when you get to your customer service aspect.

Finding this passion isn't the most natural thing to do, and for some people, it takes years before they come to discover what it is they love. Rather than waiting for all these years, you can ask yourself two questions which will help you determine what your ultimate products will be.

"What interests and hobbies do you enjoy the most?"

And the second question is: *"If you made no money, what sort of product would you launch?"*

These two questions find what you have a passion for, and with regard to the second question, it takes money out of the equation as a motivator and will leave behind the natural emotion to your products. It will also open up the bigger picture in revealing what your real motivation is, in terms of launching a product. Yes, a product that you can improve and provide; one that's better than the competitors.

A profitable niche can be around for a while, but as soon as you find a competitor begins offering a comparable product which is an improvement over yours, you might have seen there is no will or incentive to carry on. In a best-case scenario, if you have no passion, you'll see yourself starting from scratch again. So passion can help to concrete your business.

Long-Term Customer Value

Although this isn't something of much consideration to new sellers on Amazon, it is one of the most crucial aspects, and one of the more overlooked areas in business.

Once you've started looking for products to market, you shouldn't only be looking at making a short-term profit. Instead, you should be looking at the long-term for your products which will sell, and you can build a well-known brand around this concept. When this happens, you can scale your business to heights you never considered, and continually build what you've created, compared to having a product which sells loads for only a few months. If this is the way your business runs, it isn't efficient. You will also find, this is the time you hit that plateau, and your sales never increase past a certain level.

It is ideal to search for a niche which you can introduce 3 to 5 profitable products; from which you can build your brand of loyalty. All of these products don't have to make enormous amounts of profit, as the point is; this group of products is all about building your brand image for the business you have created. From this group, you might have two standout products which bring in around 80% of your profit. Nonetheless, the idea here is that once you've launched your first products and built up an email list of loyal customers, they will be keen for your next product launch/es.

For reference, it has been shown that it is around seven times easier to sell to an existing customer than selling to a new one, and this is the reason you can leverage an existing customer base above your competition when you release a new product within the same niche. To go along with this, when you release a product which is somewhat related to your others, you can use the same marketing techniques which you already have in place from the release of your other products.

To enforce this, we'll take a look at an example. If we were looking to supply splatter guards inside a kitchen niche, we should take a look at what other products these buyers have been purchasing or viewing. This can open up avenues of where to explore next, and you might notice there are abundant products which go along with splatter guards for use in the kitchen. You can choose from pan sets, chopping boards, knives, and many more useful kitchen implements.

Now, for the purposes of this example, where a customer has purchased a splatter guard, and they were on the lookout for another item, if they were presented with this item under your brand, they'd be more inclined to purchase the same brand. Usually, they want to maintain consistency of the product line because they like the brand. And, if they purchased from you before, they'll be more likely to do this again.

Overall focus should be on the business as a whole, and brand ideas compared to single items which will lead nowhere. This will open up avenues of thought of how you can group these products into building your brand. The number of products you supply doesn't need to be five, but it can be a good base on which to start, and from here you can leverage your customers and meet their needs.

Mistakes You Should Avoid

No one is perfect when they are new to any business. Actually, there are plenty of factors you need to consider, and a good few can easily be overlooked. Any new seller should learn from the mistakes of past sellers who have been through it before and come out the other end with a solution to the problem. Here, we'll take a look at some mistakes sellers make which are common ones that can easily be avoided by being aware of them.

Although typical, these mistakes can have an adverse effect on your business, and it's crucial you try your hardest not to fall into the same trap and make the same mistakes. With foresight, there is no reason to make these mistakes and end up wasting your time and resources.

Products Which are Oversized

Amazon stipulates product sizes that sellers should use as a maximum. Anything larger than this and extra storage charges will be due. Always check these size preferences on the Amazon site before stocking up. You can obtain all the item dimensions from their website, or by typing into Google "oversized products on Amazon." This also gives the charges which would be due if your item fell outside of the guidelines.

FBA fulfillment goes in-depth into all of what you should do, and what happens when you don't regard your product sizes. This can be a simple thing which is overlooked, and a product which ends up too big or too heavy will have extra charges, and these could quickly eat into any profits that you make.

Gated Categories

There are specific products which require additional checking, qualifications, and reviews before they can be fulfilled by Amazon. A product can't merely come from any supplier, and it is a best practice to contact Amazon ahead of schedule, just to make sure your supplier is a trusted one. A prime example is men's watches which are sold under the jewelry section. For this, there are additional requirements you need to comply with before selling in that particular category.

With this, it might appear to be negative, however, it can go a long way to providing protection against competition. Although you need to fulfill these extra requirements, it means they also do; now any reseller can't approach a niche and simply begin selling, not when it is gated.

Product Patents

This can cause sellers significant headaches when they are selling products on Amazon. It might be the case that their product is selling well and the business is growing. After a while, a notice is received which states the product they are selling is patented in the USA. This could lead to the product being withdrawn and the listing removed from Amazon. At this point, income will stop, and the reseller is left with unsold stock, and their storage charges will mount up.

So, to make sure you never fall for this, another Google search can be completed, this time through google.com/patents. What you are presented with is a valuable resource which you can view. As a consideration, if you are serious about your Amazon business and are at the point of investing a few thousand dollars, it might be beneficial to hire the services of a patent lawyer who can do these searches on your behalf. The cost for this could be a few hundred dollars leading up to the thousands; however, if you are looking to invest more than this, it is worth the cost, rather than seeing your business come to a standstill.

If your product is one in which you are doing the importing, it is wise to perform your own searches. Trademarks are another thing to consider during any patent searches. These are much the same as patents and can have the same effect on your business. These can easily be searched for using USPTO. Here, you can search brand names and slogans which might appear to be similar to yours, and so infringing on their rights.

Supplier Sourcing

Later, we will be going through the sourcing of a supplier. However, it is still an area that some sellers have difficulty doing. The entire process of dealing with a supplier should never be hard or overly stressful.

As an example, if you intend to sell printed pet items ready for Christmas and spend plenty of time sourcing suppliers; it can be a major red flag when none of them offer to print the collars that you asked to be printed. So, do a test first to be sure they are reliable. Check out their reviews, call them. Make sure they have a fantastic reputation.

There are more than enough suppliers around who sell the right products, allowing you to change and adapt to times like these at Christmas.

As soon as you hit some slight resistance, you shouldn't consider giving in. Instead, it should mean you are attempting to push your business onward and upward, rather than hitting a brick wall on every corner you take. The only instance where these products should be considered is: if they are highly profitable and the research you've conducted supports this. And so, it might be some-thing worth pursuing. One thing to keep in the back of your mind is; that every day you are not selling the high levels of volume you expected is another day you're losing your revenue, which shouldn't be taken lightly. This is especially true on a fast-paced platform like Amazon.

3

Designing a Brand

CHAPTER 3

Now you have your final ideas, it's now time to create that unique product from your thoughts. From what was just a thought will soon be brought into reality, and be something you should aim to make better than your competitors' ideas. This can provide your customers with a reason to purchase your product, compared to another. It is also the reason your product solves their daily problem/s.

Branding products shows your customers you have precisely what they're looking for, and why it is capable of solving their problems and holding an advantage over all the other products which are competing for their business. When you have this, it is known as your unique value position, and it is this which makes your product stand out from the multitude of others.

With branding (which is creative) you can catch the eye of potential customers who are searching Amazon using specific keywords. Yes, the ones which you have conveniently "selected" for your product descriptiveness in your title, subtitle, and description. This is funda-mentally important as it becomes your first point of contact with your customers. And in that split second, they'll take their first steps toward making a purchase of your item, and then proceeding through with the finer details. This is the reason why getting the branding right is key, it's more than a fancy design and packaging. Branding is (quite literally) the first business impression you can make to your customers.

Branding doesn't stop at this stage, either. Once customers receive your product, you need to convey the impression they have their hands on a high-quality product, and they have made the right decision in their purchase. We'll explore this further throughout the title, and in following chapters, of how you can best do this.

Branding and Your Competition

Before proceeding further, it's essential you understand what marketing is, and how it relates to your businesses branding. For me to explain the concept, we'll be using hair shampoo as an example. With nothing more than this shampoo, and if we strip away all forms of product branding, we have remaining, nothing more than shampoo in its barest form.

Without information, we have no idea which brand this shampoo is, the benefits of the product, or an explanation of the contents inside. Likewise, we can't smell it either, as the fruity smell is also a significant part of the branding of the product which remains hidden.

If we could now compare this with a designed bottle of shampoo, we'd instantly notice the vast difference. The product's information being printed on the packaging, the bottles design colors, and the graphics which provide more images of what we can expect when we buy this shampoo and open the bottle. So, if both products were placed next to each other, which is the one that a customer would decide on purchasing? Unless the customer has an aversion to paying high prices for products and the prices happen to be substantially different, the customer is more apt to choose the branded shampoo over the plain version.

This example highlights how customers feel when they purchase products, but, when it comes down to it, customers always select branded products they feel at ease with as they know what they're expecting to get from the product. Customers don't want to receive any surprises, or a product they don't fully understand. With this in mind, the more information we can present to them, and the easier on the eye our products can be, the higher chance we have of making the sale.

We can go further and see exactly the difference between the two products as a way to demonstrate how effective marketing can be. First, we can see that the printed bottle holds more volume and is of a more substantial size, and then, any further packaging gives the opportunity to add more information. E.g. Like a newly launched label, and details on how well the shampoo cleans and nourishes your hair. This is where a unique selling position of a brand comes into play.

Now, this product goes from something which was just a product which only cleans your hair, to something which cleans and gives you shiny locks. It also offers benefits for nourishing the scalp and preventing dandruff. Additional information is often included, such as directions and how you should use the product to its best effect. You will also see the placement of logos and a specific color theme. At a quick glance, customers can see the branded bottle is the one they want, and they instantly recognize it as the superior product because of its branding features.

This is the science behind what branding is, and what branding does in the eyes of a customer. The aim is getting the point across to the customer. And with some investment in market research, you can determine what it is, exactly, that your customer is looking for when purchasing specific products. It is at this stage, you can focus the branding of your product to reflect your customers' wants. This unique selling position is essential as it is where you focus your efforts on the solving of specific problems. This can easily be achieved with branding, rather than showing or explaining everything in great detail (which would overcomplicate matters and make your product confusing).

A Unique Selling Position

As previously mentioned, your unique selling position is what sets you apart from competitors. It presents your products as being better solutions to your competitors' products. This is crucial to get right. Otherwise, you might find your competition is offering greater advantages which will steer your customers into choosing their products over yours.

There are several ways you can hone your unique selling position. The first is by researching reviews on your competitors' products, and from receiving valuable information. Here, the customers are telling both you and your competitors precisely what they need and what they are looking for. They will also make known in reviews if the product did as it should in meeting their needs. Additionally, we'll also examine what precisely customers ask for, and from this, we can develop a clear, concise, and unique selling position which we're sure will meet all of their needs. Additionally, we can carry this over to our overall business branding and marketing techniques.

Now, with this unique selling position in place, we should be confident we can steer customers away from competitors and toward our product, so they'll have the confidence in making the purchase.

What is it that Customers Want?

Large companies (each year) spend many millions of dollars in trying to conclude precisely what their customers look for in particular products, or in a specific niche. It's not an easy task by any means, and it can take lots of time, effort and resources to fully understand the answer. When you're aiming to see what your customers want, it's best to make notes in the exact words they use. By doing this, you easily understand exactly what they are looking for with regard to particular products, and their experiences when using them. This method is better than using your own interpretation which would leave room for error and give results which are not precisely correct. Precision is key here.

To look at it directly, if a person stated they wanted a premium product instead of a high-quality product, you would aim to find what they mean as being a "premium" product. This could be that the product has more features, attractive packaging, and it comes with additional services or support. Higher-quality, on the other hand, might mean the product's materials are of a higher-quality, while there are no additional benefits associated with the product itself. Different phrases lead to a different conclusion by different people. The word "premium" creates mental images which can be very different from another person's. So, it's best to seize the information as you found it, and use that going forward, rather than wrongly making up your own mind, and missing what your customer is looking for.

To make sure you find precisely what your customers are looking for, navigate to the Amazon website, and select the bestseller ads. These are the best place to begin looking at products which are highly liked by customers. While searching, you'll also see that even these contain one-star reviews. This is entirely normal, as not everyone is pleased all of the time.

You'll notice both the five-star reviews and the one-star reviews are extremes, and this is what happens when people merely act on emotion. In the best scenario, it'd be they love the product and are happy to share their feelings, or they haven't had a positive experience, even if it is their fault and they wish to use the reviews as a way of venting their frustration.

The full value of reviews is found within the two, three and four-star reviews, because these are the customers who might take a different perspective when reviewing a product, and won't let their emotions get in the way of what they quote.

When you wish to begin narrowing down your unique selling position, you need a blank document to note things down. Take notes on each review and detail them in as full a way as possible. It has been known that some people like to use a spreadsheet for this task and can be feasible too, as data can be sorted much easier. This task can take a while, and maybe up to a few days or a week.

This is due to the fact that your need for exploring is quite in-depth for each review and, after a while of taking notes, you can start to see what you can do, or what's not possible for your products. When you spend the time in doing this, it can lead to a vast advantage over your competitors. Any reviews you find won't be limited to only your products, but across any branding or marketing techniques. This might include your sales and customer service performance, also. It can make a wealth of difference, so it's advised to have all of your bases covered.

You will find a number of reviews that start to say the same thing. It is essential in making this known when you make your notes (by adding a mark for every time the same thing was mentioned). Doing this can help keep track of what customers ask for the most, and it will help you get closer to knowing what your unique selling proposition will look like.

Another way you can do this is to navigate to writewords.org.uk. Here, take a look at their word frequency counter. Now, all you do is copy and paste a review into the tool, and it will make a count of all the words used in the text, and it will list the number of times words are used. Obviously, there will be words which are not relevant to the product, so filter through these and search until you find common words which relate to your products. With these words, you can gain a rough idea of what you might be able to offer as part of your unique selling proposition, and also toward your listing title. This, including your keywords and any other marketing; is key, because this is taken from the exact words of potential customers.

One thing which you might notice in the listings is: it doesn't need to be the product which has the unique selling position. This glory could be placed on the listing itself.

An example is, if we check the iPhone case niche. There are some listings which state the product is a "premium" one. This will allow the cover to stand out and be noticed above the other cases in the market. This happens as many are mass produced very cheaply and "shoved" onto Amazon.

When products are seen as being a premium product, they typically demand a higher price which will also stand out, this might only be due to marketing, but it generates a stronger perception of better quality and a more improved design. The listing type can also work the other way around, and you might find products listed which offer the lowest prices too, and this aspect is used all over, in many niches.

There is another option which many people do specialize in, and this is by possessing the most number of reviews in the same market. This can be useful for niches which don't have high amounts of reviews and are limited to around 100 and 300. Customers become drawn to these products which appear to be selling in high volumes, and which are popular, with the reviews being an informative sign this is true.

To further this example, other unique selling positions you might see include the words:

- Shockproof
- Ultra-light design
- Highly engaging graphics
- RFID blocking

When looking for alternative ways of improving your product ideas, there is one easy (yet effective) method you can use. Take a quick look at what items customers purchase together. This will give you some ideas of items which people buy in addition to the one that you're thinking of selling. What you can do is sell the two items as a package, or include accessories which make your products too good an opportunity to miss.

This technique will put you way out in front of the competition because now, rather than buying two items separately, customers choose your brand because there is less effort required and it costs less to purchase two things together as is listed on your product.

Okay, jumping back to the iPhone cover example. An excellent way to explain this point is for iPhone covers which come with screen protectors, or perhaps a stylus. It offers that extra incentive which is all you need to bring customers over and to buy your product rather than one from the competition.

Branding and Visual Elements

CHAPTER 4

This can be the most exciting time when releasing a product to the market. This is the time you decide how your product will look, along with the associated branding. One factor to note is: product appearance ranks high on customers' wish lists, and it shows how they perceive your brand.

How Should Your Products Look?

Any visual image you have will include suppliers in the first steps. Your ideas need to be communicated with them. Further in the chapter, we'll explore how to take your unique selling position from the concept stage and bring it into reality. You'll do this by using solutions which your suppliers can design, manufacture, and build. We take steps away from ideas and begin creating results which we can use as benchmarks. A pat on the back should be most welcome at this stage, as many people have already given in by this time, due to a lack of ideas or a distinct lack of confidence.

To make sure you have a product which will stand out and be unique, you need to go through listings for current products and check what your competitors are creating, just to give you some much-needed inspiration. You'll see tons of products which are generic and lack vibrant color, or design elements. This should motivate you to exploit these areas which are lacking.

Once you begin to get an understanding of what needs to be improved upon for your product, you can then put it ahead of the competition. Head back to Alibaba.com and start searching the base product for which you wish to work with. This should be the basic idea of what you want the end result of your product to look like. When you see the product listings on Alibaba, you are looking for some inspiration for what you think would be the best start to build on, on top of your unique selling position.

Save a few images which show the style and features you want for your product, and your next step is to head to Photoshop and begin editing images to give your suppliers a much better idea of what your final product should look like. The design doesn't need to be overly well done, as not all users are very good with Photoshop. To save too much hassle with communication, you should use labels to highlight the feature you desire.

If you lack the funds for hiring a designer, and you wish to undertake all of this work, just be sure to do the best you can in giving answers, and don't forget, at some point, you will be ordering a sample very soon. This is crucial to know how the finished product should look, and what elements need tuning.

From the images you have taken from Alibaba, make sure all third-party logos are removed. At the same time, you can create your brand's logo and use it to go with your images. This will now paint your online business in a more traditional and professional light.

When you Need a Designer

Rather than taking on all of this Photoshop work and attempting to come up with a logo, you can hire the services of designers from the freelance marketplace, these professionals can improve your image and make it look as you want. Try Fiverr and/or Upwork.

This is well worth the investment, and even more so if you are just beginning, as your suppliers will be returning back to you with numerous questions they want answered. These will be about the design and the specifications of your product. Typically, this is an element that most people would not have any clue about. Experienced designers can make sure all this information is in place to minimize these additional questions.

One cheap option (and one of the easiest to use) is Fiverr.com, as just mentioned. Here you can find graphic designers who are advertising their services. The prices begin at $5 and work their way up, depending upon the skill of work required. There are some advantages when using a designer in your team as you go and venture further into an Amazon business. You know from the start that you can have professionally designed logos, packaging, and all elements of your branding. You might also receive some advice on aspects of your design ideas which help lower your learning curve when building a product and your brand.

There are a large number of Fiverr services which specifically target Amazon sellers, and these are the best guys/gals you need to look out for. They have previously worked with Amazon sellers and know precisely what to expect when designing products for new suppliers.

Product Designs

CHAPTER 5

Packaging which is attractive does more than merely being a container for your product. The packaging is the central part of an extension of your branding, and unique selling position. It is also a critical element which will be seen in all your marketing efforts, so getting it right is vital.

There are elements of packaging which should be considered before looking to create the ideal packaging for your products. High-quality photos of how the product will look in a customer's hands, and how it will feel, are extremely important. The packaging materials, the packaging, and how it is looked at with regard to your unique selling position are all paramount factors here.

High-Quality Pictures

You would think that having high-quality photos might seem obvious, but, when checking product listings in your niche, you might find that a high number of photographs and product packaging is of very poor quality. Additionally, they don't capture the full element of what the product means. The goal is to make sure your product leaps out at potential customers and gains the most number of reviews it possibly can. Photographs should be used to your advantage, and by using the highest quality available to you, you can make your product really shine.

Amazon stipulates that you're prohibited from having text across your photos. Although, you can have text on your packaging, and use these pictures to display this text.

For example, if you have a product which offers a free book along with a product. Here, by using your packaging to show this offer (and it will be something very unique and something similar products wouldn't do), you can beat the competitors.

You must also be sure to provide maximum value through the choice of your packaging, and no space goes to waste. You might notice there are a lot of packages which have images which do nothing to sell the product. The pictures are nice, but they offer little value and are wasted opportunities.

When it comes to providing accessories or bonus items which are bundled along with your products, you should consider the addition of a touch of color. This will now appear in search results and will show a contrasting color, which differs from the many other products.

As a prime example, if you were selling pan sets, a lot of the color is generally silver, grey, and black. When you add a colorful accessory (such as a recipe book or potato peeler), you've taken the opportunity to add color which will catch your potential customer's eye.

Packaging Materials

When the time comes to decide on your packaging, it doesn't need to be merely a cardboard box; rather, this can be your opportunity to make sure your product really stands out.

Alibaba also has suppliers who offer a vast variety of different packaging, and much of it depends on your type of product. As a good example, if you were searching for a container made of wood; this might be miles away from what your competitors use when packaging their items.

Wooden boxes give a higher premium look and feel to them, and can be reflected in the price you set. Coupled with this, you're more likely to receive favorable reviews as this is something which surprises and surpasses your customer's expectations.

How You Display Your Unique Selling Position

The packaging you decide upon is a unique opportunity to show potential customers what it is that makes your product something unique, when compared to the competition, and why they should purchase yours as a preference. Taking your unique selling position, you need to be sure to make an effort to see that your packaging highlights your solution to a customer's problem.

This might be much more than materials you've used, or any images which are in the product package. It might be how the wording and the branding are expertly displayed on your package. This can come down to the colors used, and this is another in-depth topic, especially if your market is geared toward women.

Generic packaging portrays that the products are cheap and not made of high quality. You'll (more than likely) have seen this over and over again with the many generic brands at the local supermarket.

While products inside the boxes might be the same, or better, the impression you receive of these products is that they're not on the same level as branded products are. This is precisely why branding with a unique selling position is much more advantageous to ensure your future sales volumes.

6

Choosing Minimal Viable Products

CHAPTER 6

Now you know how you want your packaging, and how it will look to potential customers, thus portraying your unique selling position, and successfully so. The next step you need to take is acting on what you've created. This is the step which will separate those people who explore for the perfect ideas and research incessantly, and those people who are the action kind, and can implement their plans and scale their business to create successful opportunities.

You should take all of these chapters to be your stepping stones. If you find you've been pondering over ideas, and returning to the drawing board many times over, this is the time to act. You now have an opportunity with which to take the plunge. You should grab the bull by the horns and move forward with your idea, rather than revamping it and striving for absolute perfection. Once you've researched properly, you can move forward with branding.

You should take note that there is no real definition of perfection, which means it doesn't really exist. In many instances, perfection can be a setback and not an advantage in the business world. It doesn't matter which product you finally decide upon, it will have room to grow and, over time, it can improve. We'll look further through the chapter at this, and how it all fits together.

What Are Minimum Viable Products?

Minimum viable products are defined as development techniques where new products are developed and come with enough features which will satisfy the early buyers. This provides you with the chance to receive feedback (and plenty of advice) from the first individuals who purchase your products. With this, you'll gain a much better understanding of what should be, and what could be improved.

While using this technique, a final, complete feature-set can be developed after careful consideration of what has been taken from the feedback left by the product's first users. How does this affect you and your Amazon online business? It is ideal if you have your MVP (minimum viable product), and it can be released straight away, as this hurdle is one of the biggest you'll need to get over to be successful on Amazon. Not only this, but it helps define the remainder of your journey.

If you struggle with an idea, or you're unsure whether one of your products will work, this will leave you suffering from fear and doubt of your business. The best way you can overcome these hurdles is by releasing your MVP and letting the first buyers provide you the answers to the questions of uncertainty you've been asking yourself. It's that simple, really.

When you use this concept, it will allow you to be much smarter in your way of working, and will also help you to avoid pushing back any launch deadlines. This is what happens when you keep upgrading your product in search of perfection, and ultimately, you'll get surpassed by your competitors. Action = sales. Non-action = no sales.

Delaying Your Progress and Opportunity Cost

One of the significant hurdles we can all face when becoming almost ready to release one of our products is; a severe lack of urgency. If you're used to working for another person instead of yourself, then there is a good chance you have become accustomed to deadlines and working to meet them. Doing this does nothing but what human nature leads us to, and that is... absolutely hating deadlines. If this was the case and you carry these working practices and thoughts of deadlines into your own business, you start to enjoy the element of newfound freedom. This leads you to believe that you have ages to complete your project, and without you noticing, this quickly turns into a severe lack of action. Without all these deadlines or a sense of urgency in our work, our steps can become delayed for much longer than we may realize, and indeed, much longer than they should be.

The best way to view this is: by looking at opportunity cost, and although it is a fundamental economic concept, it can be used to see the value of giving something up when exchanged for something else. When you use it in the perspective of your Amazon business, this is the cost of not acting when compared to launching your MVP product and making essential sales.

To get this point across in one swoop, we'll use an Amazon business which makes around $10000 profit a month. This is realistic, once all is running sweetly, and there are a few practical steps which you can take to get you there.

Now, with this in mind, you'd be losing around $333 each and every day (on average) over a month, and when your product isn't on the market and making sales. When you use this simple calculation, you'll quickly know exactly what you need to do every day to earn what you are hypothetically losing through opportunity cost.

This means you need to quickly move to the next stage. You need to communicate with your supplier and check that everything is on track for release and supply. Even proceeding past this point in the guide can be seen as a course of action. Action = sales.

Making Incremental Improvements

You need to keep firmly in mind (even if you're not happy with the looks of your product) the materials it's made from, right down to the colors of your branding. All of this can be changed and improved further down the road.

As an example, if you ordered, let's say, 1000 units of your product, and you knew within a month or two you'd need to order again, at this point, you'd have a 1 to 2 month period where you can continue optimizing your product. Do this by analyzing feedback from your first customers.

This will give you some peace of mind that whatever you decide to release to market can be an improvement for the next batch of orders.

There is no need to make massive changes because you can start small, and improve the little things while improving your product overall, and with each new purchase. All of these can cover many areas such as: in the products, product packaging, or the inclusion of new features or bonuses.

Your products should be selling well, whichever way you go, and you have the first batch selling as your MVP all while (at the same time) improvements are being made in the background.

Will all of this in mind and in place, even once you've released your bare-bones product, to begin with, you now understand it's product quality which sells over the long-term, and you are at the stage to focus on this, especially when you know the timing is right for that product.

Amazon and the Technical Flow of Your Products

CHAPTER 7

In this chapter, we'll be going through the more technical sides of shipping products from Amazon. Each of your products must be barcoded. This occurs before they are shipped from your supplier to any of the Amazon warehouses, and then (once purchased) to your new customer's door. These labels can appear to be highly confusing for sellers who are getting started with Amazon. The thinking behind this chapter is to familiarize you with UPC codes, and to also help you become accustomed to the entire process before you are in the position of getting started.

What are UPC Codes?

The letters UPC stand for "Universal Product Code," and even without realizing it, you're likely to see UPCs on numerous products which you are accustomed to using on a daily basis. These codes have one purpose, and it's to help track products which move through an entire network of operations, from shipping, to being on shelves in the store, and finally, being bought and taken home by many happy customers.

The creation of barcodes which you'll use on your items is straightforward and inexpensive. For you to do this; there is one website which comes highly recommended and it is called speedybar-codes.com.

From this site, you can purchase UPC codes and have it quickly converted into a barcode once you are almost ready to ship your batch of products to Amazon. If you are starting and your range only covers one single product, you just need to be worried about purchasing one UPC code, at this time. Nonetheless, once your business scales, you could start buying multiple codes once your product range increases.

Submitting UPC Codes to Amazon

After you've purchased your UPC code, you now need to take the next step and submit it to Amazon. This connects the code to your particular product. To complete this, you'll need to navigate to the Seller Central home page and select the manage inventory tab.

Next is to click on the listing which corresponds to your product which you're looking for the label of. Now, select this product and click on edit (which opens a new tab where you can see the product ID) where you need to paste your UPC.

Once this has been done, you're ready to save any changes, and then head back to the manage inventory tab. Here you are to click on the drop down which is next to edit, and you'll find the option of printing your item labels. You'll also notice you have an opportunity of having your listings fulfilled by Amazon, or fulfilled by a merchant.

If you select fulfilled by Amazon (FBA), you can register your items to be fulfilled by Amazon, and from there you can choose the print item labels tab.

This option of printing your time labels, brings up further opportunities to select your label size. It's best to print quite large labels as it'll be more accessible for fulfillment and scanning.

Select and click on print labels, and download the PDF file. This is now the barcode for your product, and now you'll need to copy the information and forward it to your supplier. They should then print the barcodes and prepare the specific labels for your product.

This can speed up the process immensely for everyone involved. Most suppliers have the procedures in place to label products quickly and inexpensively. Once your products have been individually labeled, they'll be placed into larger shipping cartons to ship internationally.

This shipping carton also requires its own shipping label, and to do this, you'll need to return to Seller Central and navigate back in, to manage inventory.

At first, you'll notice it says zero available. From here, you'll need to select the drop down and choose to send and replenish the inventory. Next, you'll be provided with a second label which is suitable to be attached to the larger box. However, before doing that, you need to provide additional information.

First, you need to provide correct information on the outer size of the box. If you're unsure, there's no need to panic. As a good example, if you say you have around 100 pieces of your products which are, 10 by 10 by 10 inches, and, you're shipping 50 items in two boxes, so 100 items total, then each carton needs to be labeled to create your shipments.

What you will find is: Amazon allocates space where these items will go on to be shipped to, this they do to make sure your customers are never too far away, and that shipped products take no longer than two days in reaching them. Each shipment that Amazon makes on your behalf, you can review who'll be doing the shipping part. One of the best things about Amazon is it has subsidized shipping when using UPS, and this gives you the best price for your transportation.

Now we need information on how large and heavy the box is. For the sake of example, we'll estimate 10 pounds. Now you can calculate your shipping cost for boxes which are that size. Next, Amazon asks if you're prepared to ship at that price. Once you've accepted, you can print the box labels and fasten them to the front of those shipping cartons which may then be shipped to the corresponding Amazon locations.

To quickly summarize your initial workflow, first, you need to procure your UPC codes to identify your items. After this, submit your UPC information to Amazon to convert your UPC into barcodes for your items. These need to be individually labeled (at source) by your suppliers.

The items are then packaged into a large shipping carton which you'll supply an additional label from Amazon, and this determines which of their warehouses the package will be finally shipped to. These are delivered to the warehouse, received and placed into storage where you'll be able to see on your Amazon inventory management screen (once they are available). The next and final step is that your new customers can begin purchasing your items because they are now ready to be shipped to their ultimate location. Congratulations!!

8

Making Connections with Suppliers

CHAPTER 8

All of your suppliers should be considered as working partners in your enterprise because you will want to find ones who you can trust and not merely work with just anyone. Much of your business success will come down to how good your supplier is at producing and fulfilling your orders as you need them. If there are any concerns like: your supplier isn't well established, or they have their own internal issues, then you should avoid them no matter how good their rates of production and supply of a product may be. All through the following chapter, we'll look at all the different platforms you can use to contact suppliers, and the benefits and/or downsides of each.

An ideal supplier is one who will happily offer assistance when you are faced with challenges, and they can also assist in helping you walk through building your business as you start to scale up to more products. When you work with a trusted partner, the entire process can be completed quickly and smoothly.

Choosing a Platform to Use

On the upside of e-commerce, there are numerous factories in the Asian region, which over the past ten years or so; have begun producing an excess of products which can be found at quite reasonable prices. These factories are itching to locate entrepreneurs who are keen to be the "man in the middle," and to help move their product from their factory to the end user. This is where you come in and take a piece of the action.

There are many services which allow these factories to display their products where they can be sold in bulk, and to locate these sites, all you need to do is a Google search for a private label, and the product you are looking for.

When you perform a search you might be presented with any of the following sites:

- Alibaba
- AliExpress
- Oberlo
- DHgate
- Thomas Net
- Global Sources

The Platform Which Works for You

Finding which platform meets your needs will depend on your individual circumstances, as well as the type of product you're looking to sell. You should bear in mind that all these services aren't equal, and ones like Alibaba and AliExpress come with more protection and customer service than the smaller operators (who don't have such an established track record).

Some services also specialize in specific categories, such as Global Sources, who focus on electronic products. Although these may seem appealing for first timers on Amazon, they are best avoided for the moment. This type of product is more in-depth and can result in a lot more returns, refunds, and faulty products being shipped back and forth. It is advisable to concentrate on products of a more straightforward nature before you advance to more specialized niches.

Ups and Downs of Each Platform

Global Sources is excellent for the advanced seller as it focuses on one type of product. As just mentioned, if you are developed, they are a fantastic source. But, for beginners, it can quickly become confusing as the entire process takes much more effort.

AliExpress and DHgate are similar to each other in that you can purchase many items from China and other Asian countries. One of their primary advantages is the variety of products which they stock from varying suppliers. Along with this is the MOQ (Minimum Order Quantity) which can be small, for some products. This is advantageous as it allows trial runs of specific products which won't cost a fortune, and which allows you to move on to another if things don't work out as expected.

AliExpress is easy to use and gives this flexibility in the MOQ. One downside is the piece price is slightly higher, and there are tighter rules on customization. When you look at this, it might limit any improvements you wish to make to your product. AliExpress and DHgate also offer more generic products which can be a considerable downside when your Amazon reputation is built upon adding value to your customers. This range of generic products will limit your ability to stand out from your competition.

The largest of all these services is Alibaba, and this is reflected in their tighter controls on becoming a reseller. This means you have a higher chance of finding a reputable supplier from here than in other areas. On top of this, you can also find more detailed information on the suppliers which will help you narrow down your supplier search, and therefore, making an informed decision will become much easier.

This adds protection on middlemen who are posing as suppliers themselves, who really take no interest in making sure orders are fulfilled. Massive headaches and business problems can occur when this happens, and this is the reason a vast majority of Amazon resellers work with Alibaba, and for the entirety of this guide, it is recommended you do the same.

When you wish to join Alibaba, it takes a few minutes for registration, and you can then begin the process of communication. Before going this far, it is worth checking all the suppliers who are showing the same products within your niche. This will be looked at in-depth within the next chapter.

As you search through Alibaba, be sure you have selected the MFR option as this shows you are searching manufacturers and not others dealing on their behalf.

Choosing Your Supplier

CHAPTER 9

Once you understand each of the platforms and their pitfalls, you can narrow down your search and make a shortlist of suppliers with whom you would like to contact. This task isn't as simple as it looks, because it isn't a matter of how good a supplier seems on paper. There is criterion which you should follow in making the final decision on which supplier to work with. At the end of the day, they need to accommodate you, and they need to be reliable enough for you to work with, long-term.

As most Amazon sellers use Alibaba, we'll continue to use them for our examples. It is (without a doubt) the best platform for beginners. When you search for suppliers, ensure they have a good reputation, and that you can rely on them. Alibaba offers options which allow you to hone your search criterion, and the search engine will provide three options which should be ticked off. Two possibilities are crucial, and it's recommended you select them, while the third (in most cases) you can leave blank.

Trade Assurances

This is one of the important options and is vital when you first enter the Amazon market. This is an agreement between Alibaba and the supplier, where it puts in place a guarantee. It states that: if a seller doesn't manage to fulfill their obligations following a payment, you don't need to pay that invoice. To show this, we'll use the following example:

If the trade assurance is $15000 and your order is valued higher than this (and then it falls through by the seller not shipping the goods), you are not obliged to pay the $15000. This gives comfort, knowing you are not liable for missing orders which are unshipped. Most of the Amazon businesses won't use a supplier without this option in place.

Gold Supplier

When you select this option, it shows suppliers who meet specific criterion on Alibaba and have reached a credible gold rating. For them to do this, they have to submit all of their financial information where there is a higher level of scrutiny, and which ensures they are operating above board. Alibaba could even arrange for factory inspections to make sure they do, in fact, meet this criterion.

This option is one real sign of a good supplier as they will have been a partner with Alibaba for an extended period, and have shipped high numbers of products. The length of time the supplier has held this status can also be viewed.

Unit Price and MOQ

The final step in choosing your supplier for the product you have selected will boil down to searching the results for a product. And one which is similar to what you are seeking. The list will contain plenty of items which are unrelated, and these should be quickly ignored.

What you are seeking is a supplier who offers a product which can be improved upon, compared to a product which is very different from what they are used to. This won't only need extra instruction on how to perfect the product, but the cost will be substantially higher.

Once you find the product which is a close match, you should open this in a new tab and add them to your favorites. Next, the MOQ should be checked, along with their price. The price should fall in the middle, depending on your order quantity. Remember, if you purchase more, you want this price to drop for each item.

Information which is listed about the MOQ can be ignored in certain circumstances. If it states an MOQ of 1000 and you only want 500 for your initial order, you can just inform the supplier (who might drop their requirement and supply the lower quantity). Once you advise them you are in search of a supplier, and you could be a repeat customer, they might just accommodate your request.

Once you've drawn up your shortlist, you need to begin contacting your possible suppliers via email. Alibaba supplies all contact information, and it is advised you use a template to make sure everything is standardized.

Here is one you can use:

Dear **(Supplier-Name)**,

My name is **(Your Name)**, and my company is aiming to expand our range of **(Product-Type)** for customers across the **(Country)**. We have received several quotes on **(Similar Products)** for **(Your Demographic)** and are very interested in discussing sample orders.

The quality of your **(Product)** looks to be great, and it appears to be close to what our business wishes to brand and offer to customers across the United States, at this point in time.

I am very interested in discussing working together and wish to speak with you regarding your unit price for the **(Products)** like the attached pictures.

This would include my company branding and logos on the items and also on the OEM packaging.

Design Specifications: Any Desired Specifications **- Size, Weight, Colors, Material, etc.**

I very look forward to speaking with you. Please reply to **(Your Email)** for bid consideration. If your bid is in the region to the others we have received, we will reach out to you within a few days.

Best Regards,

(Your Full Name)

This template is formal and professional, yet easy to understand, and with the inclusion of a table with all the variants or shipping details and prices you wish to ask. Additionally, it can save considerable time in reviewing their replies.

Private Labeling Terminology

CHAPTER 10

Before discussing how best to communicate with suppliers, we should look at the terminology which is used on sites like Alibaba, and what you would use in your communications. This can be vital, as it might come to the point when you don't understand each other's comments. It is advised that you learn all of this so you'll appear professional, rather than attempt to sound professional without understanding the context of a conversation.

All of this terminology is industry-wide and not merely exclusive to Amazon specifications. It will be used in many areas and can be a thing best learned to save asking questions later.

This list covers the most basic and the most common terms. There are many others, but in the beginning, these are all you should need to understand.

Sourcing of Suppliers and Terms

MOQ

Remember MOQ is the abbreviation for the *minimum order quantity*, and this will vary from supplier to supplier and be dependent on the product. This is most often the set price which will be profitable for supplier or manufacturer to produce the given product. Anything below this price is improbable as the company won't be unable to make a profit to make such an order size that's worthwhile.

MFR

This is used a lot, mainly on Alibaba, and all it stands for is *"manufacturer."* MFR is purely an indicator that you're contacting the supplier, who is also the manufacturer, rather than a third party who might be seeking to make money from forwarding product listings. You'll need to deal with the manufacturer, rather than any third party. And since you can make direct contact in the case of problems, you should be in a position to secure the best possible price.

OEM

This means *"original equipment manufacturer."* It is an indication that the supplier has, in fact, designed and created the product which is listed. This should say you can use their tools and basically get creative with their creation. You can use your own brand and logos on their packaging, and also on the product, and this is a crucial advantage when you are private labeling.

ODM

This abbreviation means *"original design manufacturer,"* and any suppliers who have this tag can offer a higher degree of flexibility in what they can do with the products. This is because they were the product's original designers.

This will allow you to send specifications where they are then tasked with the design and manufacture (on your behalf). You can essentially create a new product, or change all aspects of an existing product.

This though, is for advanced sellers who specialize in particular products and will know exactly what they want to create. For all beginners, it's better sticking with the OEM suppliers.

QC

This means *"quality control,"* and shows products are checked and reviewed to make sure the batch in manufacture is in working condition, and up to standard, and not broken or faulty. You should seek a supplier which has high levels of quality control, as it can help avoid dealing with a high number of returns and refunds, and in the worst case scenario, you could be inundated with bad reviews. This is not good.

Trade Assurance

We showed this is Alibaba's way of protecting customers and keeping the suppliers accountable. Make sure the level set is something with which you are comfortable, and refrain from going over this figure. Always cover yourself here.

Payment Terms and Abbreviations

PayPal

This is the most recommended method, and especially when you are beginning. PayPal will allow you to send money directly to any other PayPal account holder, and it has built-in protection for both parties if sending and receiving money. Your first transaction should be made via PayPal or trade assurance, which will allow you to ease the payment process and also prevent the chances of falling victim to scams.

Western Union

Western Union is a service which allows users to send remittances to any part of the world, and by using only a person's name or linking to a bank account. This will allow the recipient (who would be your supplier) to collect funds at a location that performs Western Union services, and is most convenient for them. This compares to waiting for money to become deposited into their bank account, which typically takes some time to clear.

Western Union is flexible. However, there will be additional fees, and there are risks involved because the sending of money doesn't leave a paper trail.

TT

This abbreviation is short for a wire transfer, and with this, the funds go directly to the bank account of your supplier. This can be one of the easiest ways to make payments, but, it does carry extra costs which are generally higher than the other methods of payment. You also need to be cautious and have the correct bank details in the first instance. Most suppliers, who work long-term, prefer this method of payment over the others because there are no fees for them.

Escrow

Escrow is a third-party account where funds are held until a transaction has been completed successfully. The idea is to protect both parties until the deal has been made. A good example being, if you want to purchase $5000 of product and want to make sure your shipment has been fulfilled before you release any money. You can use Escrow to confirm to the supplier you've paid the correct funds, and that you will make it available once your goods have been received.

Escrow services typically receive a small percentage of any funds which have been held, but in the end, Escrow can work out expensive, and when you use Alibaba there isn't a lot of a point because of their trade assurance, or PayPal (which are great options). Escrow is more suited to beginners, because the higher the value of your orders, the more expensive it becomes.

Shipping Terms

FOB

This is an international shipping term. FOB means *"free on board"* and is an indication your product is heading to a port which has been previously specified. As an example, it might say "FOB Bridgeport," and this means your products will be shipped to this particular port at the expense of the shipper, from this point, you'll be responsible for customs and moving it from that port to the final destination. This would (more than likely) be a shipping company, or the use of a freight forwarder.

The alternative is cost insurance and freight. With this, the supplier would cover all the costs to get your products all the way to your location. This would be reflected in their pricing structure, as they won't do it for free.

EXW

This means "ex works," and with this, the supplier is only responsible for the manufacturing of your product. Any transport from their place of manufacture will be your responsibility. You are most likely to come across FOB, and have your supplier deliver directly into Amazon's warehouse of choice. But it's good to understand this term, nevertheless.

Supplier Communications

CHAPTER 11

Now you know the terms of what you can see regarding shipping and payments. And you will need to make the first contact with your supplier using the template (given earlier). Now is the time for your first deal, and to get the ball rolling for your business on Amazon. Although, before you do this, you should be aware business can be conducted in a very different way when dealing with overseas suppliers.

Chinese companies deal with things in a very distinct way, compared to their American counterparts, and knowing this can be crucial. Any miscommunication should be avoided so business can run efficiently. Always be polite and professional.

Differences in Culture

All Chinese business is conducted formally, so emails would be written in a very different (and not in the somewhat casual way they are in the USA). All email communication should be addressed as Mr. or Mrs. Which is then followed by the surname of the person you are addressing. Any casual opening of written communication should be avoided.

Rather than forcing communication with your supplier, you should let them lead the way so they will become more comfortable when conversing with you on a personal level.

Sir or Madam is the best opening (if you are unsure of their actual names). This also presents your business as being more businesslike, in their eyes. They will see you as a company and not only as a single person who is selling on Amazon.

Without using casual remarks or humor, be distinct about what it is you want, because in our native tongue and style of writing, we leave many things open to assumption, rather than detailing every little thing. Chinese business doesn't allow for any assumption, and they will take all that you say at face value. This is crucial, as you might be expecting a product of a particular specification, but if you haven't put it in writing, you could be paying for something you haven't even ordered. Be very specific, in every instance.

Differences in Time Zones

It is (without a doubt) going to be a very different time for your supplier, than for you. If you are based in North America, your supplier's time zone will be the exact opposite. With this in mind, you need to allow for this when expecting or sending communication via email. There could be a delay of over a day by the time they get around to replying, this is not them being slow or unprofessional, it's merely the fact they are on the opposite side of the world.

Negotiations

Western culture frowns upon bargaining to a certain extent, it cheapens the proceedings and the perception of the product. But, in eastern culture, this is expected, and you should show that you understand this in your first few negotiations with them.

Your supplier should come to understand (or think) that you are asking the same from other suppliers. This will lead them to offer their best and last price for the product. When they come back to your request with an amount, there's a good chance this is a little over-inflated because they will be expecting you to negotiate. This is where you can give them a price that you have theoretically received, and see if they match the amount you have offered them.

All this still needs to be conducted professionally, and show them that you wish to do business with them above all the other suppliers you are speaking to. On top of this, you can indicate you have a budget to work to, and if they can't fit into this, then you might have to approach another supplier.

Lost in Translation

Communication between cultures isn't always easy, and even after years of contact, things still become misinterpreted. When you are asking questions, you need to make sure they are clear and precise, and there is no room for thinking you mean something else. Unusual or slang terminology should also be avoided as you need to stick to words that your supplier will know. It is also recommended to number or letter your questions, as this can help them work through the process far more easily.

Chinese business people will say flatly they don't understand, even if they know half the question, they won't go further until the full question can be fully understood. To make sure this doesn't happen, you can lay things out in a straightforward manner and ask them to repeat back what their interpretation is, so there is no confusion. This confusion will always be there, but watching out for it can make it easier for both you, and your supplier.

How to define Your Product Samples

CHAPTER 12: HOW TO DEFINE YOUR EXACT PRODUCT

If managing your first import wasn't exciting enough, this is definitely where things will be exciting, because you're now presented with the opportunity to have potential products in your hands. Your initial product samples will be exclusively created for your brand, and for your Amazon business. This is the product you'll be shipping to your customers, so it's crucial that you have a sample product which you're proud of, and which you know your customers will be more than satisfied with.

It's crucial having your sample branded, and the finished product in your hand, as this will give you an idea of the final quality and if there are any issues which might arise. At present, you still have a chance to rectify these before your product goes into mass production, by getting a sample before you begin selling.

You already know your product has to stand out, and for it to succeed in doing this you must convey to your supplier precisely what you require from them. With this, there are so many variables which will be worked into the designing of your product, and there's a high chance things might turn out differently to what you expected them to. It is for this reason why you need to order samples so you can check, and be sure your product is the one you asked for.

Supplier Screening

You might wonder how many samples you should order, and the answer comes down to a question: how many suppliers have you made contact with about placing orders?

When it comes to creating new products, you'll want as many opportunities open as possible, and this will mean you need to talk to as many suppliers who manufacture the product you are searching for. A general rule: it is advised to contact around 10 suppliers for each new product you have, and from these 10 you can screen the possible suppliers and also gain a better understanding of the market. You will also have room to cut some suppliers from your list who don't perform in these early stages, or which you don't feel are suited for the assignment. Unfortunately, some might also be difficult to communicate with.

Sample Comparison

It is never enough to have only one sample, so you'll need to order three (at least). A number such as this would highlight any differences in their manufacturing processes, so you'll have a good idea of the supplier's overall quality.

By the time you're ready to order your first samples, you should now have a good idea which company you'd like to work with. This will now allow you to compare all of the product samples together, and to see which ones (beyond a doubt) stand out, regarding quality.

Moving Forward and Negotiation

When you have your three products firmly in your hand from your chosen group of companies then, from your short list, this can provide you with additional leverage when it comes down to your negotiations. You can run through the best points of each sample to the other suppliers and describe any benefits. You can then express that you'd like to see these particular features or design elements from their company, rather than on one of your other samples. Discuss with them the possibility that they can make it happen with a more affordable rate.

Once you've narrowed down your list and you have an excellent idea which company you'd like to work with, you should order a second round of samples with any improvements. This is to be sure the quality is the same as the first set of samples given.

Quite often, companies prepare samples with little extra care and make sure they are top quality; however, when it comes to production, things can be a bit different. The second sample would be an indication of how your product would look and feel over the long-term. This is also how it would be received by your customer, so, it's best to have a final check and be on the safe side that everything is still up to standard.

When your supplier is ready to ship your first sample, it will entail some other questions such as: how much will it cost? Where does it get shipped to? And how will it be shipped? The shipping costs for these first samples will fall between $40 and $150 for a single sample, which (of course) is dependent upon the weight.

These samples will be shipped express because there is no point in wasting time at this stage, and the shipping will be direct to your home or business. It is also crucial that you don't become bottle-necked when checking samples, so streamlining the process as much as possible is advised here.

Payments for samples should be made with PayPal, since the amount is small and won't have any substantial fees attached to the payment (as would be the case if you were shipping a complete order).

From this point, you'll need to begin working toward the purchase of your samples and running through the logistics of having this order shipped to your desired location. Your possible suppliers should have outlined everything when you sent them the template to complete.

Honing Your Company for Success

CHAPTER 13

Many people overlook the importance of this, and when it is in a guide, it is one chapter which is often skimmed through. There is importance here, and you should be aware of it as it can determine your business over the coming months, and the next few years as well.

You might be asking what all this means. As a brief example, many individuals wish to start a business on Amazon. They get tangled up in the early stages of starting the company while they are learning, and then they come to a grinding halt when they hit a roadblock in the process. When this happens, they continue and only get average returns and average success, rather than getting the most they possibly could.

Companies Which Succeed While Others Fail

If you are still in full-time employment and are seeking to start an Amazon business, there is a good chance you'll find it hard to have the time to commit to your business, which is a fair assumption. This might appear to be shameful, but it is a very natural occurrence. Working this way could leave you exhausted on certain days, and you feel you can't do anything toward your business, or you work all weekend, and then half of the following week you can't manage to do anything.

Many travel the same path, including their working practices, and it is this inconsistency which should not become a habit. From this point (and it has been proven), companies who are successful make plans of how they are going to accomplish tasks, and the ones who fail are the ones who float along with a general approach, hoping everything turns out fine. These are usually the ones which end up failing.

When you place this methodology on your own personal Amazon business, it shows that: you should have a plan and stick to it. Of course, there will be days when you can't do anything, but setting goals and planning around these off days will guide you toward your success. These plans take away distractions and allow you to focus on what needs doing, rather than merely working on something when you feel like it.

Cultivating Your Good Habits

This section is a follow-through from the previous, and you should slowly change your habits. Remember, you will be going from the employment of someone else, to becoming self-employed. When you do this, the effects are profound, and you will notice a drastic improvement in your business.

All the way through, you should set smaller goals, rather than one large one. This is because these are easier to achieve, and doing this also allows for flexibility along the way. On top of this, you'll feel happier on each goal you reach. Once you begin changing your habits, you are more likely to achieve something each day, and you'll quickly find you are more efficient in completing tasks than what you used to be.

From here you can plan to work a set amount of time, and it doesn't need to be hours on end, a straightforward hour is enough to help break old habits. With this; comes consistency, and you might find you wish to work longer, but if you set the minimum, you'll never fail.

To make sure you're focused on your work period, you should have one task which you wish to complete, rather than several. Having more than one allows your mind to wander, and you'll end up achieving nothing, although you might have appeared busy. So, do each task one-by-one.

Take Small Steps to Reaching Your Goals

At the most, you should have a maximum of three tasks you want to complete in your working period. You might not finish them all, and you can roll the unfinished part over to the next day. So, do all you can, and you will see results, and with a deadline, you push yourself to complete as much as you can in your allotted time. Make sure you allocate times for each task. Great organization is key with regard to any business.

Each section of this title is a step toward your goal. If you spent an hour reading each chapter and taking notes, it's an hour well spent, because you are moving forward. Now, you can compare this to reading it (when you have time), but you probably won't take it as seriously, and the actions that follow stand a good chance of not being completed.

Results of working in this way are that you are less likely to feel burned out through cramming work in when you have the chance, and this becomes all the more important in the earliest stages of your business.

Each day your top priority will change, although, the amount of time you spend on completing your top priority will remain the same. You learn to block out your distractions during this period, and you learn to focus your brain for that one hour. Other elements should be consistent. Include your time, your desk, and your room, which should all remain consistent. When all of these are geared up for work, you'll quickly fall into the same vein and accomplish another goal on your way toward success. Take short breaks and stay fed and hydrated. Your body needs the right fuel to sustain itself, so be health conscious in this regard.

How to Determine a MOQ

CHAPTER 14

Now you've been communicating with your chosen supplier, you should have made progress in working out a deal on the price. The next question you need to ask yourself is: what is the minimum order quantity you shall be ordering?

This question can be hard to answer in the beginning, and will be different for each person and each business, and most of it depends on your circumstances. The purpose of this section is in assessing your situation and determining what the best way is, for moving your business forward.

You must keep in mind that mistakes will be made, and predominantly in the early stages, but, this is something you shouldn't fear. You'll be faced with challenges and errors, and these will occur more times than you'll come to expect, especially when starting a business for yourself. You should know that it is the fearless nature which helps your business grow, as well as learning from your mistakes. The best way to go about it though, is by learning from others' mistakes (and not too many of your own). That's what's covered in this next section.

Risk Management

Risk management is one piece of your strategy; it's needed when making the decision of the order quantity you should be placing. Here, you take out any emotion from the equation and use real mathematics to dictate your order size, and now you can assess the situation based on circumstances, and the best efforts to maintain the financial health of your business.

Here, there will be two options you're faced with. One is for placing a smaller order quantity of, let's say, 1000 units, and the other being larger, with 2000. The more units you purchase, the higher the risk your investment faces. Apparently though, with larger orders, you should make higher profits because the items would have become cheaper, and as an aside, these larger volumes help to reduce shipping costs.

Correspondingly, you might be faced with items which are a struggle to sell, so you could find that your investment might take longer to pay for itself, if it ever does. Even with clear research, the market can change and have highs and lows.

If you have a product which you've never sold before (and this includes deciding on your first order size), you might feel some apprehension in getting your feet wet with such a large order. However, keep in mind how it looks to your suppliers. They deal with orders of magnitude every day, and if you only place a small order of up to 500 units, your supplier won't value your business to the extent of a buyer who is placing orders which number in the thousands. But never go over your budget, either. Your stability is first and foremost.

Fear is a barrier which prevents us from taking action, and in business, this fear is a hindrance more than a protective instinct. To be honest, mistakes in business are really only there to help you, to help you learn and grow as a person, and as professional.

If you are willing to take your business seriously, you'll need to put yourself on the line, and with that comes tons of commitment.

Second to this, with the knowledge that you've gained so far, such as idea and product selection (and product innovation), you should have the insight and faith that your product is going to be successful. If this isn't the case, then it shows you still have a lot to learn. You will also see that you'll continue to learn through the many challenges of business. So go easy on yourself.

Low MOQ the Pros and Cons

When having a low MOQ, it provides you with the flexibility of needing a lower initial investment in the beginning. There are also downsides to ordering lower quantities, such as a higher price per unit. While it might not appear as if it is much of a problem, especially when you're paying less for your first batch, you'll quickly decrease your profit margins on each sale. Overall, this will affect the success and longevity of your business, so do the sums to be sure.

When you make less profit, it means you have less to reinvest in your second order, and this leads to the next order not being as big as you'd like. Bear in mind that you're not your supplier's only customer, and they'll have hundreds of orders to fulfill each month. Now, when you are placing small orders, they won't take you very seriously at all. Just be aware of this fact.

Many people feel that having lower order quantities prevents them from running a risk of holding too much stock, especially if their product doesn't sell as well as expected. In some cases, this might be true, but you're setting yourself up (and even waiting) to sell less stock than you want.

To fully understand this, let's reverse the situation. Let's say your product sold very well, and you quickly ran out of stock which went on to create backorders. Now customers must start waiting for your product. This might take weeks for you to fulfill their order. This causes your business (and your Amazon rankings) to suffer "big time." This can be extremely dangerous and is much more detrimental to your business than if you are holding unsold stock. If we look back at the opportunity costs of not having your product on the shelf when it comes to making money, we can see the high costs of not being "market ready."

High MOQ Pros and Cons

When you have high order quantities, it might appear as though it's a higher risk of your initial investment. Although it does have a higher number of pros than cons, these cons are few and far between. Actually, there is the risk of purchasing a product which doesn't sell as well as expected, as we've discussed previously. It might take longer for a return on your investment, but it's unlikely that you'd make a loss on your products overall, especially if you've done your research homework at the outset. Remember, you would've spent the first part of this title in the area of research, for products which would work with those specific and "workable" formulas that were discussed.

If you carried out your research correctly, and you've got the confidence to bring your product to the Amazon marketplace, you should find no reason not to buy a larger (minimum order) quantity.

Also, you'd circumvent any risk of running out of stock if your item sells better than expected. All of the returns from your initial sales allow you to proceed with further orders, and to make sure you have stock delivered before the current inventory has been sold. Lastly, this places you higher up on your supplier's ranks as a preferred customer. A higher MOQ for your initial order should total around 1000 to 1500 units, and no quantity less than that (unless you decide it's necessary for budget reasons). I would like you to be confident in your research skills, though. Take more time if you aren't feeling confident in that regard.

MOQ and Calculating What Works for Your Business

As we stated at the beginning of this section, your MOQ varies depending on individual circumstances, which are that of your product and of your business budget. There is a quick way to calculate what sized MOQ will work for your company, and present you with a clearer picture of risks and rewards for each overall shipment size.

You can calculate your inventory turnover quickly by: taking an order size, say 1000 units, and divide this number by the number of sales you expect to make each day.

As an example, if you're selling 20 units per day, your inventory turnover would be 50 days. This means, after 50 days (at these figures), you'd run out of your product stock. If you don't, you should really have a good idea how long it takes for your shipments to arrive at the Amazon warehouse, and know it well, before it can be dispatched to your customer. If you find this transport time is longer than your inventory turnover time, then you'll run the risk of depleting your stock before the next shipment arrives.

Another factor to consider is: how much it costs to ship each item. This varies as it is dependent on item size and weight. Consequently, if you're buying smaller items, you have much greater flexibility in ordering a more substantial number. If your items are rather large, you might want to consider ordering smaller amounts, just to begin with.

There are other variables involved, and the lead time from your supplier is definitely one of the most crucial aspects to know. If you don't order soon enough, and they have a lead time of weeks, you can run the risk of depleting your stock. When you add together all of these factors, you should have a reasonable estimate of what the best MOQ for your budget and risk is. You can then make adjustments accordingly. Don't forget, perfection is purely an illusion, and mistakes and errors which add to your overall costs can be rectified somewhere further down the line. Try and work out possible problems before they arise. This is called "having foresight," and it matters in business, very much.

Managing That First Product Import

CHAPTER 15

This is the start of really serious and exhilarating times! Your business should now be in operation, and you've placed your initial order. Now it's down to your supplier to be awesome at managing your first order fulfillment, and this is the time where you'll need to maintain your levels of communication, just to make sure your supplier is keeping up their end. You also need to keep yourself updated to ensure your first import runs as smoothly as expected.

You should be aware, this isn't the time to sit back and think of the money rolling in, it's time to be serious here. Now is the time where you'll need real discipline and to be focused. This is because there are more people involved than *only you* in the equation. For one thing, your supplier will be expecting you to be available in case they have any questions or problems which need to be tended to. When these arise, you need to make sure you have established a method of communication which is far faster than email.

Methods of Communication

There are many ways you'll be able to communicate instantly with your suppliers, apart from sending emails. We now live in a time where communication is simpler and more straightforward than ever before. You can send instant messages and receive replies within minutes. This allows for fast communication and the chance to do business faster than ever.

In this section, we'll take a look at the ups and downs of each method of communication. The primary methods we use on a daily basis are email, Skype, and WhatsApp, along with some other ways.

As we mentioned earlier, Chinese businesses operate with a much higher level of formality than western companies, and for this reason, we first need to start with email as the chosen communication method. We use this to first establish our working relationship when we first make the important contact. The Chinese have high regard for formality.

From this first communication, you can loosen up slightly as you work to become more familiar, and go on to start to grow comfortable working relationships with one another. The reason email is the best form of communicating when first making contact is that: as your level of accessibility and regularity increases, with this method of communication, the overall level of formality drops.

Email isn't considered the most convenient method of communication, nowadays. After a time, you can ask if they'll use other methods. So, apps like WhatsApp are designed for faster and more frequent contact, which means all discussion will end up being more casual over time.

Aside from them being convenient, another consideration you need to make is the ease of tracking communication and documents. With email, this is simple, which is why it would also be the best to use in the beginning. With added search and tagging functions, you can segregate all communication with your suppliers.

As you further build your business relationship with your supplier, you can begin to use less formality. When this happens, you can then use more accessible and convenient communication with methods such as WhatsApp and Skype.

Every method also has it's time and place for being used. Skype is great for working through lists of instructions or details, and the chance to have a face to face meeting, which requires direct attention. Finally, there is WhatsApp which is very similar to Skype, yet quicker to use in more situations which need faster responses (such as getting your shipping labels or giving a fast answer to an important question).

Email

To start, email is essential. It provides businesses with high levels of formality and the chance to appear professional, which is difficult to portray when you are using instant messaging apps.

When you use email, it will allow you to track and categorize conversations with your supplier. Documents such as invoices can be attached and archived (for ease of location) when using the search function to find something from earlier on. Email is a slower process which allows both parties the time to respond at their own pace in the beginning, and while these parties are still getting to know each other.

WhatsApp

Once you have become more relaxed with each other and both parties are used to direct communication, you can start using an instant messaging service such as WhatsApp. This will allow you to keep in constant touch with your supplier much more quickly and more frequently (just don't forget the time difference). The major downside to WhatsApp is that there is a lack of tracking in your conversations, which means it can be hard to recall messages or essential documents, which is far more suited to email.

Additionally, if you were to message through lists of questions, it might be harder to receive a response because WhatsApp is geared up for shorter messages. This is another reason you'd be better off emailing larger communications, instead of trying to use WhatsApp in this regard.

Skype

The middleman is Skype. When you slowly downgrade the formality, and you are more comfortable with your supplier, you might want to consider conversing with Skype. With voice or video conversations, you can ask questions and receive immediate answers. Issues can be worked through at convenient times with the time difference, and the conversation will mean much more than short messages on WhatsApp, or having a long delay for a response via email. That's unless it's for documentation purposes. Use email for documents and files.

Page Ascension and Its Principles

CHAPTER 16

Amazon's page ascension principles are an essential set of knowledge guidelines, which is vital for any Amazon seller or entrepreneur. It is the expertise in these page ascension principles that can mean the difference between your new product ranking higher up, or falling down and being hidden a few pages in. And, most of all, not getting as much attention as it deserves.

Page ascension is decisive, as every single product which is launched will start somewhere near the bottom of any search results for a specific term. This is down to the fact that it is a new product, and it's never been sold on Amazon before. With this in mind, it's impossible for Amazon to know whether your new product is relevant for any of the given search terms.

There are rules with which you can follow that will allow your product to climb through the rankings and reach the upper levels of search results. This can be one of the most stressful and time-consuming areas which you will study on your journey to becoming successful on Amazon.

Density of Keywords

These keywords basically search terms which you will insert into the text on your product listing. This will allow Amazon's search engine algorithm to take a customer's search keywords and see how they relate to your product listings. For example, if a customer searches for a potato peeler and you've used the keyword "potato peeler," dotted around in your product listing, this is more likely to show your product listing than if you weren't using these keywords at all. The frequency in which you use these keywords also has an impact on how the search engine locates your product listings. On top of this, the location in the listing can now also play a part in your rankings.

It's ideal that you'll have your chosen keywords to target precisely what potential customers are doing searches for, and this is a reason why this keyword density is *unbelievably* significant. This will be covered in more detail later, but for now, we'll briefly cover the basics. Your title is the first *and one of the most critical parts of the puzzle* which Amazon takes into consideration when doing a search. When you have a title which matches the significant keywords a user is searching for, this is one of the essential things to make sure of, so your listing is reaching the top of the page.

This can be closely followed by any bullet points you have, and then your product description. It is crucial to optimize your keywords through your product listing, so they match the ones which are being searched for. All this is crucial in getting your product ranked higher, which in turn, leads to a higher number of clicks from your page. Keywords and keyword density should never be underestimated.

Rates of Conversion

Conversion rates are what tell the Amazon algorithm how many visitors there are who will actually click on, and then visit your product listing. This goes on to if they are then buying the product they have viewed. This is an excellent indicator which shows that the person searching has (indeed) found what they were looking for, and that it was located in your listing.

If you have been using the keywords for "potato peeler" when you are trying to sell a garlic press, you would very quickly find your conversion rates are way down, and because of this, Amazon's algorithm will adjust your product listing to show lower in search terms which are ranked with potato peeler, mostly because it's been shown that there is no match to the search terms.

When you look at optimizing your conversion rates, you can adjust some of the variables which are shown on your product's listing page. You can split them up, and then test how the alterations work, compared to the first attempt. Doing this, you will see which method of optimization works the best.

You will come to notice conversion rates are affected by keywords and search terms that you have been using on your page. This is because the number of visitors to your page is (overall) determined by how well and effective your search terms will match up with the keywords which are being entered by potential customers.

The better and closer the match, then you'll get more clicks, and if these keywords and search terms are firmly related to what your customers are searching for, you'll naturally receive more conversions. This is key.

Sales Volumes

Your sales volumes are one of the most significant pieces of sales ascension you can have for your product listings. This is made up of both your actual conversions and your overall keyword density. The more optimized your listing becomes with Amazon's search engine algorithm, and the higher your conversions are, the higher the number your sales volume will be.

There are numerous ways of how you can increase your overall sales volumes, and it is mostly a result of the previous two elements included in your page ascension.

It is for this reasoning that it's vitally important to make sure both your targeted keywords and your conversion rates are highly optimized as much as possible, as this can become the defining factor in the number of overall sales your product will experience on its listing. Look at other products that sell well in same categories. What keywords are they using, and in what density?

Optimizing Your Product Categories

CHAPTER 17

Now you are at the stage where you have a product, and it is beginning to sell. So now, you can start to figure out where in Amazon it fits best to make the most significant impact on customers. Finding the best place on Amazon is crucial as you will now be competing with other sellers. Choosing a category sounds simple, but there is much more to it than that.

Amazon does have some say in which category you belong to, this makes it all the more important to make sure it's correct, the first time around. You will know if you are in the wrong one as you will not make any sales because no one can find your product listing.

Conversion rates will suffer, and your business will end up in a sorry state and not at all healthy. On the flip side, if you get it right, you'll see conversion rates go through the roof, and you could eventually win the invaluable seller tags.

What is it that goes into choosing a category? We know you need to be found by your customers, so you'll need to be in a category which best describes your product for a start, and if possible, you want to be in the category which makes the competition easy to deal with.

Niche Categories

One way to make sure you advance your product is by choosing a niche category where you want to become a major player in, in simple terms, you want to be the "big fish" in the "small pond."

Your goal here should be competing with others, but at the same time facing the least amount of competition. You will see that most significant categories are over-saturated and hard to compete in. This means you need to look for a smaller one. Now you need to try and choose a category which isn't so competitive, although you need to make sure the category is still highly relevant to your new product.

You should never be afraid of leaving a significant category and entering into smaller one. As long as the category still describes your product in the right context, a lot of customers will still locate your product when searching for your keywords.

Sellers Tags

On Amazon now, there are some "new release tags" (these are also termed either a "#1 new release" or a "hot new release") for products which have an excellent sales history in each of the categories. You don't need to have made the best sales figures to get these tags (there is a "best seller" tag), but it's very likely that you will be in a position to earn a "new release" tag.

You might be asking how you get these "new release" tags. You should remember: when you pick a smaller and much less saturated and competitive category, you are more likely to be awarded this tag. This goes a long way in helping to increase your traffic and also the sales which you make as a result. In turn, you will also see your conversion rates increasing. It is ironic, but your product doesn't need to be exceptionally new to earn this "new release" tag. On Amazon, there are no definite rules for what qualifies as being "new."

You should also make sure to avoid the use of misleading tags. Some people add fake tags on their products in an attempt to boost sales. At the end of the day, this isn't allowed, and secondly, it will make their product appear worse than it is.

You should never feel the urge to compete with sellers who do this. It doesn't help, and at best, it can hurt their business. Don't let it hurt yours.

Finding the Ideal Category

To choose the ideal category, you need to log into your Amazon Seller Central account. Navigate to the catalog, and select *add a product*. Now you are given several options, and one is to categorize your product.

Either you can browse a list of categories, or you can perform a search for your product name, and then see which categories Amazon suggests.

Once you've located the relevant categories, open up Jungle Scout and search for those categories to find out which ones are selling the least. Now, these categories with which you can compete in easier (compared to one of the major categories), and with the right keyword optimization, you might find you have a first-page product.

Do remember though, your product might not fit into some categories at all, and if one is chosen which is too different from your product, your product might be corrected by Amazon. It is also worth noting that some subcategories fit into two main categories.

Also, you should not forget there are some categories which need approval before you can list products. Health and personal care (or jewelry) being two of the main ones which require approval.

Selling inside these categories can be a trade-off; they might be less competitive, but you'll need to wait until you have permission to list products in these specific categories.

Additionally, you need to remember your goal is in helping your potential customers to find what they need. You won't be doing them (or yourself) any favors in attempting to play the system. This is the reason to try and pick the correct category which matches your product. It is for your customer's sake, also. In the end, all of this reflects well on you, your brand, and your sales. And sales = money!!

Product Descriptions

CHAPTER 18

For your product listing, it's time to determine what your customer wishes to see when they have located your product, and to also decide how you are going to market your product to them.

In this section, we'll see there are several parts to a product listing page. One of the main elements is choosing optimized keywords in describing your products, and you'll see how these keywords do most of their work in the background. Another crucial factor is to use the same keywords your competitors are using, so we will also look at how you can achieve that too.

Another section of the product page is what customers will see, this is your title, description, and any bullet points. Here, you need to be descriptive without being overly technical, and above all, you need to keep an element of being personal with your customer. Being human in your description is far better than appearing like a company who doesn't care much.

Reviews and a keen price are other areas in which we'll delve into a little later on.

Choosing Your Keywords

Keywords can be found by looking at the competition's titles, and as long as they haven't used a brand name, there's nothing wrong with using their titles as your keywords.

You should also look at any bullet points they have on their page and use these as keywords in your titles. You will also find you can easily copy and paste these into the relevant sections.

All of these can be used. However, it is still the drop down box from the search which shows what customers are looking for. In the drop down you might see synonyms (descriptive alternatives), and many of these are common among sellers, so it's important you use these also. As well as these principal terms, there are others like the second and third key terms and, if at all possible, you should attempt to fit these into your keywords.

Keyword Inspector is a tool which you need to purchase credits to use. So, once you open an account, you'll see it is an invaluable tool because the keywords that products are using don't necessarily always show up on Amazon.

To use this tool, log into your account and head to the reverse ASIN function. What you do here is to find another seller who is selling a product such as yours and find his ASIN number. When you enter this into *Keyword Inspector*, you can see the keywords your competitor is ranking for. Here, all you need to do is note the "most viewed" keywords.

You might be concerned you have too many keywords, but you should be aiming for numbers in the hundreds. As these aren't shown to your customers, there's no worry of your customers becoming distracted, and all they do is help your product be demonstrated well in any search results.

Many sellers say Amazon only uses a particular keyword once; if this is the case, and it is debatable, use as many keywords as you possibly can, rather than using the same ones over and over.

Optimizing Your Keywords

At the time of choosing keywords, you need to draw customers in, the ones who are looking for your products. This leads to higher conversion rates, and remember, your conversion rates are determined by how many people buy your product after viewing it. It's no use having lots of views if nobody buys your product.

Consider a product in a niche. As an example, we'll use a blanket with a picture of a baby playing with a dog; you might have to optimize keywords for "blanket" and "baby." Most people who are looking for blankets will need something which is much more understandable. "Blanket" alone is nowhere near enough to make your blanket stand out from plain blankets.

Additionally, people might not be looking for a minor aspect of the product. If they search for "baby" and "blanket," they're more than looking for an actual baby. They might, however, be looking for a baby blanket, so it's important to optimize the word "baby" as a keyword here. There's no point in attracting one type of customer with basic keywords when they need another other product, so make sure you add the secondary keywords to differentiate your product from others.

To put it all in a summary, you don't merely need the highest number of views as possible, what you need is as many views as possible from customers who will want to buy your product. So, all real keyword optimization allows for is: as much as weeding out people who don't want your product, it also continues attracting people who do want it. The best of both worlds!

Creating Your Titles

When you create your first title, and you'll see as you go on, it will be one of the most significant things you do to help your product. First, your title displays your product to potential buyers. And remember, there are many different ways of saying what a product actually is. Here you can use any term you wish, but attempt to choose words which explain both the item and what the object does, or as an alternative, use a combination of two different terms.

It is also advisable to use verbs and nouns in your title, so it sounds natural, while still being descriptive. For example, "Soft and Squeezable Exercise Ball and Stress Relief Tool" is a prime example of a title which both explains the item and also explains what it does.

The second thing is: your title should possess some keyword density. Amazon will chiefly index your title as well as indexing the keywords. You need plenty of keyword density. The easiest way of doing this is to make sure your title is mainly comprised of keywords with no irrelevant information. Keywords should be placed toward the start of your title as that is where the search starts, and the second half of the title should serve as your product description.

Titles should also use natural language and not be robotic when spoken, or entail keywords which make little sense at all because this is of no use. The title should be understandable and accessible to read for customers, and you should use correct punctuation and then you'll end up with a more explicit title.

Don't forget, these are real people who are searching and purchasing, don't ignore this, because you should cater for them, and not only for Amazon's search engine.

Furthermore, you should make it very clear in your title: the unique selling point. For example, you might say your product is far better than many others, or it can work along with other specific items. A unique selling point for your product can be anything you like, as long as it isn't that your product is the "cheapest."

Lastly, you need to be sure to check everything, and don't make simple errors which are easy to avoid. Check spelling before publishing because it's not easy to change your title later. It looks really messy if there are spelling errors.

Product Descriptions and Human Connections

Once you have decided on your fully optimized title and all your keywords are laid out, you're now ready to proceed to your bullet points and your product description. This is straightforward and easy to do, and won't take a massive amount of time to complete.

The use of bullet points is to highlight your unique selling point. When you see a list of bullet points which are formatted appealingly, it is easy for customers to divulge without overloading their senses. You can try and use icons or emojis, or plain checkmarks as your bullet points to help raise the appearance of your list. Be sure, though, to check they display correctly or you'll need to change them on Amazon.

When you are writing the content of your bullet points, you shouldn't spend a significant amount of time describing your product's specifications. Make sure to write persuasively and inform your customers of why they need to purchase your product. You should look at making a human connection, rather than merely explaining what your product is and what it does.

In the product description, you now have the chance to write a more in-depth piece of information. Not everyone reads this as they already know what they want, but, it's crucial to cater for the people who don't know or scour every bit of information. You should also include a couple of sentences about your company as well as your product. Once again, you're aiming to make that human connection *which is crucial*. Your customers should be made aware subconsciously that you're trustworthy and dependable, and a company which employs real employees who actually care.

Pricing and Reviews

Written reviews and your star rating relate profoundly toward your product description. Like your description, these are the first things potential customers look at, nevertheless, unlike descriptions; you can't just add these things yourself. It is ideal for your product to have at least four and a half stars, with twenty (or above) written reviews.

We'll see in a while how you can increase your reviews, and also your ratings. For now, though, remember you need to have them in place to put your customers at ease and make them feel comfortable about buying from you.

You should also consider the selling price which your customers will see, and you don't want to be the cheapest as this cheapens your product. On the other side of the coin, you don't want to be the most expensive either, because if you increase your price too much, fewer people will make a purchase and your conversion rates will fall.

Remember, before moving on, reviews and pricing are the first things customers look for and see. These are as crucial as your product title, description, and your keywords. So don't let these slip.

19

Product Listing Images

CHAPTER 19

Once your description is written, you can start thinking about images for your product. There's more to pictures than just taking a picture with whatever device you have at hand. So, we'll talk about composing photos and setting the stage for a great image.

You'll want an image which displays your product in the best way possible, and by showing off its great features, too. You'll also need some secondary photos. Your images shouldn't rely on effects or be overly-designed; the product should speak for itself.

All this is easier said than done. Of course, you might choose to have an image professionally taken, so we'll talk about that as a serious option which will make your vision even better. You can also use stock images to save money. There may be a temptation to save money further by photoshopping images, but that's something that you really shouldn't do.

The bottom line is that your images should be a serious investment. Images are one of the things that will really draw in customers, so you shouldn't scrimp on photos when you do them. So, let's look at how to get the best you can, and as much as you can when it comes to photos.

The Main Image

An excellent first impression is essential to make, and your product images are a crucial part of making that happen. You'll definitely need to include pictures of your product. Amazon makes it simple and straightforward to upload your pictures. However, it can take time in creating an eye-popping decent image. So, you should give a lot of thought to the images.

Your product's picture should stand out and be unique and different to all the others. You don't necessarily need to use a still shot of the product, and it makes sense to have an image of your product in use. If you supply that your product comes in different colors, you should set the default as an eye-catching color.

Images on Amazon should be as large as possible, although you only have a small square in which to work, so you should make sure the images take as much space as possible in their designated area. You need to also make sure your image is in high resolution, so when customers click on the image, they can see it in all its detail.

Never use a phone camera to take your images, always use a proper camera, and if you edit the photos, only perform minor touch-ups. Remember, "a picture paints a thousand words," so you'd better make sure your photograph does justice for your product. It's fun too.

It is advised to have a professional take your product pictures, or if your product is already on the web in other areas and in circulation, there might be high-quality stock images that you can purchase.

Secondary Images

Amazon allows up to 6 images for you to use on your product's listing page. You should (ideally) use a diverse mixture of still images and images with your product being used.

On white background images are good, this is because they display your product as it is, and it's important for customers to be able to see all the features of your product. For this reason, it's good to have a close up of your product from a couple of different angles, and be sure all of your product's feature parts are displayed.

Lifestyle images are pictures that show off when your product is being used. It's vital to show your product in actual use, and please don't use Photoshop to compose a fake background for your product in use. People want to see your product being used, and as an aside, if you show the product in use, avoid showing things which aren't included. To summarize, photographs are one of the most critical investments you can make, so take the time to make sure you get the best images to work with. The picture is what the customer looks at first.

20

Launch Day!

CHAPTER 20

You're now at that stage and almost ready to go live with your new product. Here, I'll show how you can build that all-important momentum during your first launch. Now is the time you'll be creating a snowball which grows in size and launches you at top-speed...

During this part of your initial launch period, you'll need to accumulate as many sales and reviews as you possibly can. You'll find it's all about reaching out to people you know, and in using your close connections.

First up, we'll show how you can use coupon codes and some discounts to attract new customers, and in return, you'll make your way onto the bestseller ranks and show up toward the top of the search results by giving out deals. Yes... in exchange for that precious customer feedback! We will then show how to get the most reviews, which we have seen are another draw to customers, as many people trust what other customers say (more than anything). We'll see how you manage to make all this happen by following Amazon's rules.

At the start, this might come with a cost associated with it, and you'll be spending money again to gain your sales and receive your reviews. Once you've had your launch, you'll be working non-stop to maintain your new customer base and a precious sales rate that you've built.

Snowball Launch on Amazon

To fully understand how the Amazon sellers manage to reach the bestseller ranks, it's crucial to understand the concepts associated with a "snowball launch." This snowball launch is merely an accumulation of first sales which can propel you toward the Amazon bestseller ranks.

First, you'll need a lot of initial sales, and you'll want to spend money, time, and resources at the start to get your product selling. You'll need to stump up some money before you sell any product, and don't be expecting to make a profit at the start.

The goal here is in making plenty of sales which continue to build, just like a huge snowball. In an ideal world, you should be receiving between 5000 and 10000 sales during your initial launch.

After your first couple of weeks (after your launch), you'll find you enter a quiet phase, and you'll more than likely not be able to increase the daily numbers of your sales. When this happens, you'll be working hard just to remain in place.

You'll have to rely on advertising, and other things to make this happen. It's about keeping up some steady and continuous sales over the long-term. But before you should concern yourself with that, be sure about focusing on your initial launch.

Launch Factors which are Critical

Two of the most critical (initial) launch factors are your sales and your reviews. As we've already shown you, the initial sales will determine the magnitude of your "snowball," and how far you can climb toward the top of the Amazon bestsellers ranks.

Marketing Your Launch

CHAPTER 21

As your launch sale goes on, you'll need to think about other ways of making sales and gaining reviews. You'll have already used discounts, so we'll take a look at some alternatives. First, we will take a look at creating ads in the correct ways and hone in on them, so you're spending the right amount of money.

Amazon supplies a great ad-model which lets you bid on advert space, although, you only pay when the ads are clicked on. When you combine the correct keywords and ads, they can bring in lots of extra sales, and all this is valuable in the period during (and immediately after) your launch phase.

After this, we'll look at how to make sales from your social media circles, which will include family and friends (among the many others you are connected to). This will also include the setting up of an online storefront if you have the chance, and this can be a temporary thing just to get your product viewed. Wherever possible, and whereever you can reach, you should ask for reviews while offering something in return.

PPC Ads

These are crucial in increasing sales and helping to increase the size of your launch snowball. When you set a PPC ad on Amazon, you need to establish a daily budget to work to. So, as you only pay when the ads are clicked on, you might not use all of your daily budgets, apart from this, some visitors will click the ads and be taken to your product.

A good starting point for your budget is $100 per day, and this you're free to raise and lower (depending on how much you can afford to spend). All this isn't lost, as you can expect to make some of this back from your sales, even if it means you don't make a profit. Spending this amount on advertising is a small amount to pay if it brings in those initial product sales.

Amazon always shows revenue from your ads in dollars. However, this won't allow for what you've spent on the ads. It will be down to you to calculate any profit that you manage to make. It is more important that you check the percentage which is shown by Amazon. This will tell you how much you've made and how much you have spent on advertising.

When you bid on ad space, this determines where your ads will be shown. Generally, each ad costs one to two dollars for each ad space, but the cost does vary. Amazon has around four areas where ads can be shown, and each has its own price.

With your ads, you have automatic or manual targeting, so you can choose between the two. Automatic collects data and suggests keywords for your ads, so Amazon is, in effect, doing your marketing and keyword optimization for you, but at a cost.

Manual targeting is where you decide the terms to bid on, second to this; you have the choice for your ad to show for a keyword or a phrase. It might seem worrying that you are not getting a return on your advertising costs; you shouldn't be concerned at this stage as it is all about getting your product noticed, first and foremost.

Obtaining Reviews

Your gathering of reviews is the second crucial part of building up and maintaining your snowball effect. Although, remember these reviews won't get you ranked higher in Amazon's search. What they do though, is help increase your conversion rate, and the people who look will buy your products more confidently, and more often.

One of the best ways of gaining reviews is by spreading the word to your friends, family, and your immediate community. Amazon is tightening its rules, and they are becoming stricter, and now they don't allow reviews from family. With this being said, it shouldn't be hard to find people in your social media circles who are willing to provide you with product reviews.

The secret is only giving your product to people who want it, and not to obtain too many reviews at once. Even if you only manage to gain five reviews to start with, that's better than no reviews at all. Over a period of time, you can steadily reach your milestones where you'll have tens or even hundreds of product reviews.

Don't worry too much about the numbers of reviews you have. Focus more on finding people who are actually interested in your new product. You can now use any network you've built around your social media, and you can search for other social groups which are relevant to your product, and join them too. In these groups, you can then offer your product at a discounted rate.

Be sure to also look for the demographic of people who are typically interested in the product. If someone shows interest and asks about your product, give them another discount. Be very creative and make sure to personally interact with people at every opportunity that you can. You should now be self-reliant when it comes to social media, because this word of mouth can spread the good news about your amazing product.

The more people you can interact with, the higher the number of people you can ask to leave a review for your product. However, as long as you don't necessitate people leaving reviews, it's okay for you to ask for one. All you need to do is be helpful and charitable with your product discount, and (ever so politely) offer the customer's option of leaving reviews.

How to Leverage Existing Customers

All the connections you have at the start will help, so be sure in building lists of people who are already your existing customers. It isn't crucial if you have a current online store, or only several customers from sites like Craigslist, but each and every connection can count. You should offer those customers a dedicated discount code for your new product, and you'll slowly build a base number of devoted followers and repeat customers, thus increasing your sales, and increasing the size of your "snowball."

Purely offering regular promotions and generous discounts to pass onto customers is one other way of receiving more sales, and you can then take this a step further, and offer deals for your customers who refer friends.

Tell all your customers that if their referred friend refers another, they can also receive a discount, and if both of them go on to make a purchase, they'll both receive higher bonus discounts.

It's ideal that you should be contacting all these people by email, and not via social media. People tend to be slow in responding to social media, while more likely to respond to a well-crafted personal email message, and one that looks professional.

We'll take a much closer look at how you can take full advantage of your social media, but for now, your social media's effectiveness is somewhat limited. You'll find it's best to use your social media in contacting customers if it's your only option, or because of the fact you've already got an existing social presence with lots of followers.

It's important to remember you should always be personal and credible. And when you are offering a great deal, you'll be turning your existing customers into a much larger and loyal customer base. Even from one contact, you can generate some further sales. Be sure that you follow up with them, and offer additional enticing discounts for future products, all the while "politely" asking for reviews.

Your Social Media

Your social media circles can be useful, but there are a few downsides. It is very time-consuming when you are trying to build a social media presence, and this is mostly because of the various numbers of social platforms around today. So, you'll find that it's not going to be worth investing too much time and wasting effort in running a social media profile just for your business.

Most of this is down to the fact that social media isn't as valuable as some individuals might say it is. Unfortunately, it has become over-saturated, and people are fed up with businesses bombarding them, on what should be a platform to contact their friends and family.

This, of course, means: if you don't already have a following, don't use it. But, if you have a significant and successful social presence, use it and exploit your contacts and followers as best as you can.

The case might be you personally don't have a social media presence. To get around this, and instead, you can make use of other people's social media. Find someone who has a thriving social account, and offer to pay the host for plugging your product (or the placing of an image of your product) on their pages, and this can also include a discount code.

It is best to let them propose the price, and if you can afford to pay what they ask, then do so. Otherwise, it might be up to you to make them an offer. This strategy will work much better with larger groups, when compared to individuals, but there's no point in being afraid to ask. It can be far more time effective and lucrative than trying to attract followers all by yourself.

Maintenance of Your Marketing

Once you have launched and you're now running into a few weeks of selling your product, there are a few things you need to keep an eye on to maintain your sales. First up; is, of course, you'll need to monitor the numbers of your sales, and you'll also want to watch the numbers of four and five-star reviews you're managing to get, along with any negative reviews you might receive. Along with both of these, you need to keep an eye on checking on your sales rank, and your goal (at this time) should be in reaching the top 10000 to 5000 of sellers.

If any of your numbers begin to show a decline, you should return back to the strategies which we've already covered. Double up on your PPC advertising. Keep issuing product discounts to a higher number of people and be sure to make the best use of your existing customer base. If you find you don't have enough reviews, you need to give further and better discounts and also much better incentives for customers to carry on leaving reviews.

It's always crucial to attempt new ways of getting more sales and reviews. Be very creative and be sure to take full advantage of any personal connections and places within your local community. The ones you might have access to, which are suited in helping increase the numbers of reviews. At this stage, you should be trying all you can to maintain what you've already accomplished. Let's keep that snowball running.

Taking Good Care of Business

CHAPTER 22

Now that you're successfully shifting and selling your product... you've now become a real business!! Congratulations to you!

But there's a lot more. You need to declare yourself as a business and complete all the necessary paperwork. You also need to think about paying taxes.

There's a good chance you'll be thinking about a trademark for your brand. If you are managing to sell internationally, you'll find there's even more you'll need to do. All of this is a hassle, and to a certain extent, you shouldn't be wasting time doing it when you should be marketing yourself.

But now isn't the time to despair, because you can get this done quickly. We'll now take a look at the path which has the least resistance for you to become a registered business (most simply). We'll also see how you can organize your bank accounts, and make doing taxes easy when it's time.

Business Structuring

At some point, you're going to need to structure and make sure your business is registered. This isn't as complicated as it sounds. When you first start a business, and you're not selling a lot of product, you haven't got much to do regarding this.

There's no need to incorporate or register yourself as an LLC; you can do this in the future. All you need in the beginning is to be a sole proprietorship. This is a legal status which gives access to various business services and practices.

When you are a sole proprietorship, you are allowed to get an EIN, or an employment identification number. This allows you the reporting of your income, and to obtain benefits such as a business checking account and a business credit card. A sole proprietorship will enable you to use the Amazon tax services. This gives you all you need to help run a successful business on Amazon.

It's straightforward to register for a sole proprietorship, and if you go to the state's Department of Revenue, you can find directions on how to complete the process. Most of which can be completed online. Instead of searching your state's website, you can just Google your state and "sole proprietorship," and you'll be directed to the registration page.

Furthermore, a sole proprietorship will apply to any business you run. So, even if you sell outside of Amazon, you'll have something of value when you register for your sole proprietorship. This is one element you should do as soon as you see your volumes increase.

If you need assistance to register for a sole proprietorship, you can use LegalZoom or Nolo, who carry out the registration on your behalf. You need to complete a few forms, and they'll check them then forward to the relevant agencies. You will then receive your completed documents. These sites are great time savers.

Trademarks and Patents

Patents can help you protect intellectual property. If you introduce a product which has a new feature that's never been seen before, you will patent those features. For many of the products on Amazon, these are the same as others sellers, so a patent won't be required.

Trademarks protect logos, slogans, and brand names. It's good to know that nobody can use any branding you've created. Being truthful here; you probably don't need a trademark, either. At the start, you don't need a trademark, but if you begin making several thousand dollars a month in profit, this might be an appropriate time to do so.

A brand is worth nothing unless it is recognized and you've done the marketing. So, be sure to focus on your launch, and focus on maintaining sales and reviews. On top of that, focus on your reaching out to old and new customers, and to make sure you're running a quality business, overall. Always be professional in your dealings.

Income Tax

Nobody likes to pay income tax, but we all need to do it. Remember, if you're paying taxes, it can show you're making money!

There are ways which you can save time when doing this, and some straightforward things are: getting a business checking account, and a business credit card. With this, you don't need to go through any personal accounts to figure out which payments and receipts are private, and which are for your business.

Once you have your business account, you might want to sign up for a PayPal business account and then redirect Amazon and PayPal to those accounts.

You can hire someone to complete your taxes for you, and a personal accountant can save a lot of time, although there is a cost. A separate way is using a service like Greenback, and with this, you can automate your tax filing. Many services cost, but it can be worth it when they show you what you can claim as expenses, and what you are able to use and re-invest when running your business.

International Sellers

You don't need to live in the US to sell on Amazon.com. You can check a list of countries where you can sell from, and if you live in one of these, you're permitted to be an international seller.

There are a few things needed to be an international seller. First, you need a US-based phone number, a mailing address in the US, and a US bank account. You can obtain a phone number through Skype, a US address with myUS.com, and a US bank account at Payoneer.

All this comes with a cost, but, it can be a worthy price to pay to participate in a market as large as Amazon.

In turn, you could set up business via LegalZoom. This can save a lot of effort. Just contact them, and give them the name of your company and provide a little more information, and they can do the rest for you. Time saved here can be enlightening; I think that's the best word.

Costly Seller Mistakes on Amazon

CHAPTER 23

We will now examine several of the most common mistakes Amazon sellers make. All will involve not accounting for various factors which will put untoward demands on your business operation.

When you ignore these elements, the significances which occur can be harsh. You can lose placement in the search engine, your sales will be hit, and you'll cease receiving new reviews which all results in failing to attract new customers.

This is the area many Amazon sellers fail in making progress, and which causes long-lasting and catastrophic effects on business. This puts a seller at the great risk of having to put an end to their business. This is down to the fact they can't see further than these challenges.

As you are a beginner, it's artful in addressing these matters before they happen, and so that you may guide your business in the right direction.

When you're faced with the additional stress of finding solutions to possibly crippling difficulties, this can be a decisive factor in wanting to grow your business. You can see there is too much at stake like: independence, flexibility, and your profit margin.

You shouldn't decide to quit too early, but instead; fight to keep your business healthy, and to eradicate factors which can possibly overpower you.

It takes too much effort in regaining any successes when you've already lost them. Keeping momentum is both crucial and critical, and when you don't plan time wisely, you might lose daily profits which you could've brought in...

Instead of facing challenges head-on and remedying them as they present themselves, it is best to avoid them altogether and this can be done by being aware of them beforehand. Let's look at some now.

Depleted Stock

Amazon's system informs you when you're running out of stock, although, it doesn't forecast flawlessly as their system is antiquated and (as yet) has to catch up with current demands.

Each day you spend with no stock, you'll lose daily sales income. Don't look at the number in stock, account for the quantity you're selling. If you're selling product quickly, you have less than the physical numbers which are showing.

This problem is the same for numerous Amazon sellers who fail to predict how fast items are selling. This oversight can cripple businesses, and thus affect rankings, reviews, and can also create chaos on systems which are in place. Up to and including the ones which handle your orders and shipping.

Keeping in Front of Demand

You might think there is more time to order your product than there is, but as your product comes from overseas, you need to place orders up to weeks in advance, and well before you need the products.

There are various shipping options available outside of sea freight, but these carry hefty price tags.

Irrespective of this, you should be working to the slowest shipping methods at first, and 30-day shipping isn't uncommon. In some circumstances, you might end up with one-week shipping, but this depends upon the product and order size, as well as cost. Once you become experienced and deal with your supplier regularly, you'll start to gain more accurate figures and timeframes, which helps in calculating your stock ordering times.

As an aside, if you have a shipment which arrives too early, you might incur extra storage fees when it arrives at Amazon's warehouse. In comparison, this would be much less worrying than having no stock on hand. Having too much is better than not having enough.

In addition to shipping times, you'll need to account for manufacturing times of your products. You're not the only one purchasing from your supplier, and they might run out of stock if there is high demand. Sometimes, suppliers won't start production until orders are placed, so you should allow for a 30-day production time, at first. Or ask them via email.

Working Example

You can do rough calculations which will account for these factors. When you determine daily sales, you need to take the average of several days, or weeks previous. This formula tells you the time you have left before ordering stock:

(Remaining stock ÷ daily sales) − (production time in days + shipping days) = days left to order

For example:

(1000 in stock ÷ 25 daily sales) − (production 10 days + 14 days shipping) = 16 days left to order

Another calculation shows what it costs you to be out of stock:

Daily sales in $ × (profit margin ÷ 100) = cost per day

For example:

$1000 daily sales × (30% profit margin ÷ 100) = $300 cost, per day

This means; for each day you have no available stock, you're losing $300 in profit. If you ran out of stock and it took two weeks (14 days) before your next shipment, you could lose out on $4200. This doesn't take into consideration the damage it does to your business by having no stock or backorders. It can lead you to be out of operation, thus affecting rankings and creating a bad impression on customers.

To help with these situations, you can use Amazon's "Fulfillment by Amazon Revenue Calculator." This hand tool takes into consideration Amazon's current rates, and also gives you the chance to enter your own prices and costs which can include: the costs of storage, labor, packing, and shipping.

When you have an understanding of this formula, it allows you to put records and alerts into place which tell you when you are running low on stock, and by making sure your next batch arrives in plenty of time to meet your customer's demands.

Marketing Mindsets

CHAPTER 24

You now need to sustain the rankings you've gained over a period, and channel them into your long-term sales. This allows you to distance yourself from sellers who are only dabbling in selling on Amazon, and to become one who is serious. Yes, serious in creating a brand around their products for long-term profits, and also scaling growth toward a supportable brand and business model. For this, you need to account for both traffic, and your conversion rates.

Why Sales are Important

Making sales is vital because it governs your conversion rates, and since Amazon will make money each time you have a sale, they're keen to rank you higher if you can make more sales. Amazon favors products which are making high sales and places them higher than ones which achieve inferior results.

Both Amazon and you will have plenty of reason to increase your conversion rate and rank you higher in their search results.

Traffic is one conducting factor, and making a high number of sales is seemingly a good thing for both you and Amazon, but the number of sales you make is determined upon how high in

Amazon's rankings you're placed. So what do you do to escape this cycle?

This is the point where the conversion rate becomes crucial. Sales are noteworthy somewhat, because they bring in money. Nonetheless, there's more to marketing than just this. Your conversion rate is how many of your page visitors make actual purchases, and there are numerous ways of increasing your conversion rates.

So, making sure you always have stock, receiving excellent reviews, supplying customers with excellent customer service, and the creation of ad campaigns are all crucial here.

You'll see that your conversation rates let both Amazon and you know the effectiveness of your marketing, and if you can put your unique selling point across to your customers.

When we speak regarding marketing, we're not only talking about advertising. Instead, your conversation rates mean your entire product listing, along with efforts outside Amazon. When all these work together in drawing customers toward your product, your product will be selling effectively.

So, the higher the numbers of customers who purchase your product as a percentage of how many have viewed it, the higher your conversion rate. This means your product has met their needs through your marketing efforts.

Let's look at how your conversion rates and traffic volume counts toward your Amazon rankings.

Example:

Conversion rates can be calculated with this equation:

Number of daily visitors ÷ daily sales × 100 = conversion rate (%)

In this example, a 50% conversion rate shows: if your page receives 10 visitors, 5 of these viewers will make a purchase.

A new seller might have a 10% conversion rate, and this would mean they get 10 visitors, and 1 will make a purchase.

However, if you're receiving 10 visitors and only selling 3 products a day, a new seller might be well-established before joining Amazon, and seeing 500 visitors and selling 50 items per day. The new seller could be ranked higher, despite having a lower conversion rate than you.

If page traffic is low, this means people who might be interested in your product can't see it. If this is the case, you need to find the reason why they do not see your product. You might have to increase keyword and search engine optimization power, PPC campaigns, or more external advertising.

If conversion rates are low, this means your product is being seen, but viewers aren't interested in buying it. This; you also need to determine why, and you should consider a price change, improve your product description, and/or imagery. You need to make it all the more appealing to viewers.

Profit Margins

Profit margins determine how much you can adjust things to attract more people to your product. This can help increase your traffic and conversion rates.

Profit margin can be calculated with this formula:

Gross profit ($) ÷ sale price ($) × 100 = profit margin (%)

As an example, if you make a $30 profit on an item you sell for $100, you have a 30% profit margin.

Figures show around one-third of Amazon sellers work around a 10 to 25% margin, while others can obtain a 25% to 50% margin. Depending on your product and product costs, any margin in this range is reasonable.

We all want the highest profit margin because this gives more flexibility in pricing (should more competitors enter the market), or if a drop in your conversion rate happens.

A suggested price you sell products for is: no lower than $20. When you're dealing with products which are cheaper, it requires higher volumes to be shifted.

Customers' VIP Service

CHAPTER 25

One crucial area is customer service which we'll examine here. You'll see why it's so important in communicating with customers, and the reason why reviews are so essential. After this, we'll see how to turn any unhappy customers into happy ones.

Why Customer Service is So Important

Customer service is one element which really does reflect on your business operations as a whole. When you provide outstanding customer service, you'll be rewarded with glowing reviews and "word of mouth" endorsements. There's also a good chance these loyal customers will repeatedly buy from you. All of this goes to vastly increase your total sales count. And sales = $$$

In the beginning, you'll more than likely provide your customer service yourself, and this is purely investing your time, and answering any customer questions. Once you've become a success and are attracting many more customers, it might be time to consider hiring a dedicated customer service assistant (virtual assistant) for this task. These are easily found on freelance sites similar to (or like) Upwork. These can interact with your customers at your request, along with other menial tasks which take up your valuable time.

Review Value

When you aim to provide excellent customer service, you also have a chance of asking customers to leave feedback on your page. When they receive good communication, it can make them more obliged to leave positive feedback. These reviews are essential for numerous reasons. First off, good reviews help increase your rankings on Amazon.

Secondly, goods reviews mean customers are more likely to mention your product verbally, or via their social media avenues. If you have acquired customers who also run a business (not on Amazon), they might need to purchase several of the same product later down the road. These can be loyal customers who can radically improve your sales figures too.

It is for this reason; each interaction with your customers should be a positive one. Likewise, if someone has left a negative review, you should attempt to reach out and see if there's a way of resolving their issue.

Turning Unhappy Customers into Five-Star Reviews

In most cases, you only interact with unhappy customers when something has gone wrong. If items arrive damaged, or it has been lost during shipping, you can send replacement products.

If you participate in the FBA program, then Amazon would reimburse you for lost or damaged inventory, only if it was their fault, though.

Furthermore, if you happen to receive negative seller feedback which has nothing to do with your service as a seller, and it is a product complaint, Amazon might delete the negative feedback for you. Contact them directly for this.

Customers might mistakenly rate your product, instead of your service. If this is the case, you should contact Amazon, and ask them to fix the problem. On most occasions, it's easy to calm an unhappy customer by just paying attention to their concern and replacing their item (if that is what the problem was).

Customers also lead busy lives, so be aware that moods might be negative in some instances. Customers have the luxury of changing their reviews, so do all you can to get them to do that for you.

26

Strategies for Reviews

CHAPTER 26

Seller feedback and product reviews are two very different things. And although they are simple to understand, they very often become confused.

Feedback for Sellers

Seller feedback is a review of your services as a seller, and nothing to do with your product. This will account for your shipping speed and customer service quality. You should aim for five-star ratings, as long as you can deal with disgruntled customers.

Seller feedback is coupled with these star ratings and helps customers decide to purchase from you, above other sellers. Seller reviews aren't displayed from your product page, and instead, they show up when a customer selects the "x item from $..." link on your product's listing page. They then select the "x% positive" link which sits beside your name.

Additionally, seller feedback pages are displayed identically with no regard to which product a customer accesses your profile from. This means your seller feedback is shown across all products, and even ones which are unrelated.

Reviews for Products

Product reviews are only specific to the product which is listed on the page where the review is located. These product reviews are entirely unrelated to your service, and if you see any which are, you need to contact Amazon and reach out to fix this. So, if you are selling a product that has many other sellers, you will share product reviews with your competitors.

However, if you're working in a niche where nobody else sells similar, you must make sure you have a good product review. Product reviews are the first thing that viewers notice. It also means you can rank higher in their search results. Remember, you don't need an entirely unique product to become the only seller of it; all you need is to have a unique listing.

Product reviews also let you know which products are worthy of being stocked. If your product receives a host of negative reviews, you can't fix that product. However, you can refrain from selling it and begin selling an alternative product to "save your bacon." Make sure you are happy with the samples from your supplier, first.

Changing Seller Feedback to a Product Review

Amazon will only send emails out asking for seller feedback. Because of this, it's up to you to find other product feedback. One way of doing this is by running an email campaign tool using various tools within it. There are some paid tools like FeedbackFive and Feedback Genius which have been proven to be highly effective, and which automate these email campaigns for you.

You can also find some free tools like AMZFinder, although they might come with some restrictions. AMZFinder allows you to send out a maximum of 500 emails every month, at no charge.

You can send emails manually, but this is highly time-consuming, and when a customer posts seller feedback, you can thank them, and ask nicely if they'll write an additional product review.

If they accidentally wrote in the wrong section, you can help them by quoting their review and asking if they could copy and paste the review to the correct place. Be sure that either you (or your customer service representative) thank them again for all of their trouble.

EBC and Increasing Conversion Rates

CHAPTER 27

EBC: What is it?

EBC (Enhanced Brand Content) is additional content about your product. Amazon limits by default what you can include in your product listing. You're also restricted to small images, and limited text formatting. When you utilize EBC, it means viewers can see more about your product and company. This, in theory, is likely to increase your conversion rates.

Strategies using EBC

There are a few techniques you can use with EBC to improve your product listing page. One is: you can add a longer detailed product description. If this is so, you might want to hire the services of a copywriter who can write a vivid description.

Large pictures are another thing you can do, which shows you're producing in a much clearer light from every angle. This helps potential customers see more of the product detail. This will help enormously, as these potential customers can see if your product is what they actually want.

Finally, you can include more detailed information on product features and specifications. With this; viewers can quickly compare your product against others, which in the end, might be the deciding factor.

The crucial thing is: this EBC should appeal to your audience. This EBC content should deliver a boost in sales and conversions, regardless of what you do. It makes your product professional and more appealing compared to others.

Trademarking and Why it Might Not Be Worth It

Amazon has made EBC a little harder to implement than it used to be. They now require you to apply for EBC, and it will involve asking for a trademark or brand registration. This though, means Amazon is on your side and will protect against sellers who attempt to impersonate your brand. As a result, your product should be seen earlier in search results.

It should be noted: any brand registration and trademark aren't worth doing unless you have a successful product on your hands. For this reason, wait until you have one or two successful products, and focus more on generating sales before applying.

PPC Ads

CHAPTER 28

Here, we'll see how to run ads on Amazon, and the types of ads that you can use, including how ad pricing models work. We'll also see how keyword targeting works, and how to determine how profitable your ad is.

Advertising is an essential component of selling any product. Advertising allows you to communicate the unique selling point of your product to a broader audience, rather than just relying on them to come across your product organically.

There are many methods of advertising, each with its own pros and cons. Amazon offers its own built-in advertising platform which provides flexible and powerful tools to create your own campaigns and run them for as little or as long as you like, based on a budget that you are financially comfortable with. Advertising, however, is not a license to print money. There are intricacies and essential elements that require consideration, knowledge, and skill to be able to utilize these effectively.

Setting Ads Up and Maintaining Them

At this point, you'll need to access the Amazon Marketing Services site to set up your ads. You'll be presented with three options of how your new ad will be displayed. As a general rule, you'll use two of the possibilities which will show advertisements that are based on keywords. These options fall under the "sponsored product" ads and also the "headline search" ads.

A sponsored product ad is shown below products, and can be run on a day-to-day basis. These ads are based on keywords which customers use to search for a product.

For example, if you're searching for a fishing rod, any sponsored product ads running, are now shown under products that the viewers are looking at. This type of ad is excellent as it meets the viewer's search requirements and offers suggestions on items they might be interested in finding.

The headline search ads will be displayed above products, and are run over an extended period. These come with a much higher budget requirement for the ads (around $100). These products are more targeted toward what customers are interested in, rather than items they're searching for. This type of ad is great for grabbing the attention of potential customers and directing them to your product pages.

Amazon runs their ads on a PPC (pay per click) model, which means you only pay if someone clicks on your ad. Amazon also prevents your ad from showing, once your budget has been reached.

The PPC model will reward ads which are effective at grabbing a customer's attention. This means when your ad is generating a high number of clicks, your cost per click becomes cheaper than when it only produces a small amount of clicks.

Strategies for Advertising

Amazon can run an automatic campaign at your request, and with this, you don't even need to choose any keywords. Amazon uses the power of its search engines, and will collect all the required data. It's difficult to know what people search for, so, this is a fantastic advertisement option for beginners. The downside of this is: you have no input on the ad campaign.

Opposite to this is a manual campaign you run yourself. This is up to you what keywords you'll use for your ad. Further to this, you can use negative keywords, which prevents your ad being shown for specific keywords. This can save money. Fine-tuning any ad campaign will take time and effort, but they can make money in the long-term.

Profitable Ads: What Makes One?

To find out how successful and effective your ad is, you need to carefully watch your ACoS (advertising cost of sale), and you can quickly calculate it by using this formula.

Advert cost (\$) ÷ sales (\$) × 100 = ACoS (%)

For example, \$75 spent on your ad ÷ \$1000 in sales = 7.5% ACoS

Amazon supplies plenty of information on your ads inside your account's pages, and reports can easily be downloaded as a text file (.csv) where you can import it into a spreadsheet. Now you can sort the data by ACoS and see which ads are the most profitable, and you can assess your advertising strategy, including the effectiveness of your campaigns as you go along.

Lower ACoS results are more profitable than high ones, and if your profit margins are equal to your ACoS, you'll break even. Any ads which are higher need to be discontinued. With any which are lower, you should increase spending to maximize their visibility.

Amazon ad campaigns should be continually tweaked, and because Amazon provides lots of data, there's no reason not to optimize your campaigns. This is mainly because: every day you don't maximize your ads, it will, in fact, cost you money.

29

Sales Funnels

CHAPTER 29

Here we'll take a look at how you can broaden your horizons with your storefront and channel people to and from websites (apart from Amazon). This concept is that of a sales funnel, and as you'll see, Shopify is the first storefront that any seller should consider as an addition to Amazon.

Shopify can be expanded by using plug-ins and is a fantastic complement to Amazon. When you have access to multiple channels of directing traffic toward your store, it allows you a broader chance of capturing many more potential customers. This way can be a more complicated method of acquiring customers compared to just offering them the opportunity of finding you through Amazon's search engine.

Why Diversify?

Amazon is only one of many ways of attracting customers. It generates and provides access to a lot of traffic. But it's not the only way potential customers should have to locate your products.

When people use Google to see you, they should be presented with as many sites as possible where your product is located. A more substantial web presence will rank you higher in Google's search results, so keep that in mind. Aside from this, it gives your business and products more credibility.

Broadening your scope also gives you access to a more reliable source of traffic across diverse mediums. If one source fails, and traffic goes down, you'll still have other sources which continue directing traffic toward your products, and thus maintaining a high ranking. As a plus, you have flexibility on these other sites which Amazon doesn't present to you.

Sales Funnels and How One Works

The process of a sales funnel is where customers who are sold on your product are directed to the location where they can buy it. Every step toward enticing a potential customer is reliant on another.

A sales funnel is constructed to direct a customer's activities toward your product, and by the way of your choosing. As an example, if people locate your Shopify store, you can offer them the chance to sign up for promotional emails, and then provide a sales code and inform them to use that code on Amazon. In this way, you get all of the benefits of selling on Amazon with FBA, without having to compete with other Amazon sellers.

How to Utilize Shopify

Shopify can come in and make things much easier and more efficient. There will be a monthly fee, although you get a free trial period. Signing up to Shopify is easy and requires minimal information. All they need is your email, a password, and your business name too.

The same product description and details can be used as you have on Amazon. As well as this, you should perform search engine and keyword optimization in addition to just reusing the descriptions you have already used on your Amazon page.

Shopify can also automate much of these selling processes, and is user friendly because: it allows you to choose varying themes, enables the generation of your shipping labels, and allows you to select payment methods which your store will accept.

You can quickly get started using Shopify with their 14-day trial; which should be more than enough time to get comfortable using it for your store. Using a Shopify store allows you the chance to fully utilize Google's search engine, compared to just using Amazon's.

Using Plug-ins

Shopify offers the use of many plug-ins which, for example, can help advertise coupons, and allow you to upsell (or make use of) a sign-up form for email addresses of potential customers. And these plug-ins can help to give you other ways of attracting potential customers and convincing them to buy from you.

Privy is one of the most useful plug-ins you can install, and it works by making pop-ups show up, with coupons advertised which customers can use in exchange for their email addresses. There are numerous plug-ins found in the Shopify catalog, some being free, and they can make your storefront radically different, and take your product in directions that Amazon (alone) cannot.

Squeeze Pages

CHAPTER 30

Here we'll learn all about squeeze pages, where we can see what they offer your customers and, most of all, what they can do for you. We'll also look at how to make a squeeze page as appealing as possible.

What Are Squeeze Pages?

A squeeze page is a web page which promotes special offers such as a discount on a product. It is used to target potential customers, and here the offer is made in return for their contact details (such as their email address). Squeeze pages can be a lot more useful than advertising or using a basic social media presence.

The word "squeeze" is chosen because the content should be enticing and the offer "hard" for customers to ignore. Make sure the squeeze page doesn't appear intrusive, and that it is as appealing as possible. The request for info should be limited; because the more time it takes them to fill in, the less likely they will be to do so.

Creating your Squeeze Page

Squeeze pages can be built on your own, so, try avoiding pop-up windows, since they will be blocked by ad blockers. When creating a page, you should follow a few key practices.

Keep the majority of what you can see in view, so there is no scrolling down. Be sure to use the word "free," rather than "discount."

Even if you offer the same thing every day, make it seem as if it's a limited-time offer to pressure your audience into signing up.

There are a few plug-ins you can use to make squeeze pages on various sales platforms, blogs, and other social networks. Most come with a cost, but do offer free trial periods. OptimizePress is a Wordpress plug-in, and then there's Leadpages and AWeber which can be used as a tool which can also perform your automated email functions. Shopify has plug-ins like GemPages and Zipify Pages, along with many others.

Where You Use Squeeze Pages

Squeeze pages should be the first thing customers see, but, it should be non-intrusive also. This is the reason: the best option has a landing page which presents customers with an excellent, honest offer.

In turn, you can have a squeeze page display a little after the page content has been viewed. In this case, it will be a pop-up which is displayed in front of the content. Even though they might be irritated, they've seen the content, so, your customers are sure they're on the correct page.

Facebook sometimes disallows landing pages and pop-ups, so a squeeze page would be competing with other content on your page. In this case, your only option is displaying a banner ad. Your ad should be shown as obviously as possible, and be almost impossible to miss. Be sure to use squeeze pages wherever you have a social media presence, search engine rankings, ad space, and/or a possible storefront. When you offer promotions in as many places as possible, you'll convert as many customers as you can.

Inner Strengths and Weaknesses

CHAPTER 31

You might not be surprised to hear that each of us has certain areas where we are good, and there other areas where we fail to make any progress, no matter how hard we try. This is something which you shouldn't to be too concerned about; it is the way human nature works, unfortunately. The crux is when we come together as one; we can utilize each other's strengths which allows us to achieve the impossible.

If you have already begun an Amazon business, you could have already spotted areas where you have made very little advancement in progress, while in other areas you exceled during the early stages of your online career. If you "hit the wall," so to speak, and thought that Amazon wasn't for you, don't rush into quitting just yet, it might just be the case of hitting a personal bottleneck.

This bottleneck can be defined in one of two ways. It can consist of time, and it can be down to finances (money), and when this plateau is reached, it might appear there is no way forward.

So, we will look to find your weaknesses, and also the areas where you are a human dynamo who can't seem to put a foot wrong! We will see how we can take this and use it to your advantage, and muddle through the hard part and watch as your incremental growth begins... again.

Your Inner Power

We all possess inner superpowers, and it isn't an "out of this world" sort of power. It is that (in some areas) we can do things without much conscious thought, and we find them easy. At this stage, we need to find what your powers are and how we can tap into them.

To do this, you need to ask yourself four simple questions, and these are:

1. What are you naturally really good at?
2. What skills do you possess which can easily be transferred into a world of business?
3. In what tasks do you excel in; when other people appear to struggle? And what do you feel the most comfortable doing when you answer that?
4. If there was only one area of your business you could choose to work, what would it be? And, if it had to be one area which you could work to make your business a success, what would you choose?

As with any questions you ask yourself, you need to be brutally honest. Any lies which you think mean nothing will come back to haunt you, because it might lead to your business failure. And that's not something we ever want.

To be sure you're receiving your best and most honest answers; you should answer these with your heart, rather than your head. The answers from the head will give logical reasoning and will be based upon experiences. Answering honestly on what you feel is right, is best, because you'll tap into that inner power which you possess.

Any answers you come up with will be unique to you. Even if two individuals were asked the same question, their gut feelings would vary, and this is the reason why we all have these inner powers which vary from person to person.

When you can offer your business the access to these powers, you'll show dedication and passion, which leads to things becoming more fun and enjoyable. The tasks which you find hard, are often down to tasks in which you feel more fatigue (physically and mentally), and which adds to the challenge of pushing yourself to make sure you can get them done.

When you are searching for this power, don't presume it will be a crucial part of your Amazon business, or it is what success and failure are resting on. Results will speak for themselves in most cases, and you can take the remainder of the work and: either outsource it or automate it to make it much simpler.

Superpowers and the Importance of Unlocking Them

Any business needs to reach the next level when it comes to revenue, and yours won't be any different. For the majority of sellers, this can be a very difficult stage of their business. Also, at this point, there are many sellers who have no idea about how to move forward.

When you take a look at your passion, and the areas which you easily excel, you can find areas of your business where you can apply a laser-like focus as a means of scaling your business to the next level.

Once you have the basic systems and processes in place, and these are allowing your business to harness a healthy profit, it is time for you to improve, and hone the skills of what *you* are best at. You'll find this won't be an overall solution as there will still be areas of your business which need attention, but when you step back and look at these areas, these are the ones which you can outsource.

Being a 'jack of all trades' can be a handy trait to have. But, in business, it means your focus and talents are diverted, and not focused where they can best be utilized. During this time, if there are areas of your business which you find you aren't that good at, or you don't enjoy them, you shouldn't be worried. Outsourcing these tasks to someone who is good at them can be a great answer.

Each person only has a limited supply of energy during the day, so if you wish to spend it on the tasks that you are best suited to, you'll quickly see you'll receive the best results. As a prime example, if you spent around 10% of your time on many various tasks, you'd quickly become exhausted and burn out before the end of the day.

As an aside, you'd see you hadn't covered much ground during the day as you were busy doing everything else. Instead of working in this way, it's more beneficial to channel your energies into areas which won't drain you as much, and you'll see there will be a dramatic change in the amount of progress which can be made.

Lastly, if your focus is on something you excel at and enjoy doing, the level of your results will be much higher, and of a greater quality than the tasks which you were dragging your feet to complete. These better results would also be achieved faster and in a more efficient manner, thus, allowing for greater growth.

32

Bottlenecks and Overcoming Them

CHAPTER 32

Before you can attempt tackling any of your business bottlenecks, you should identify what (and where) they are. For many, this task can be difficult if they look at their business as one entity.

This is where it is broken down into the two distinct sections, as previously mentioned. Money and time are what every business in the world is built upon. If you are in a position where you have more than enough of both, you'll find you're in a far better situation when it comes to scaling your business, than if you were lacking in either of these areas.

Time

For a person in business, they're more likely to focus on "time wealth," rather than money. The reason being is; that this time wealth allows entrepreneurs to focus on business and have dedication in building the fundamental elements of their business. Time wealth is already in abundance, and it's down to the individual person on how they choose to spend their time, to capitalize on their output.

Even though time might be in abundance, we spend our time

completing many various tasks. Although we all have the same 24 hours in a day, some individuals have commitments which require most of their time and attention. This will limit the amount of time in the day that can be spent running and building the business.

These commitments can be studying, family, or possibly working in a full-time job to cover expenses. Conversely, we might have an excess of time, but, if we're not using it as efficiently as we could, this can be to our detriment.

If you spend lots of time resting and recharging by watching TV, or taking long naps or engaging in recreational activities, you might need to consider prioritizing your time toward your business more. This is especially true if you don't have access to a vast deal of money wealth.

Creating more time wealth is straightforward. Take notes on a typical day, and if you have a job, then merely highlight this time as taken, because you won't be able to build any business during regular working hours. Next, take a look at the time that you have free at the end of your day. What do you do for fun, and does it contribute to areas in your life you wish to improve?

There's nothing wrong with watching TV, but if you're struggling to find time for your business, it'd be wise to give TV a rest, at least for now.

Once you've managed to free up some time, you can then allot this as business time, and by giving the TV a miss for 2 hours, you've already increased your time wealth.

Financial Wealth

When we talk of wealth, this is what most people think of, and it is financial wealth which is the foundation of success, in many cases. For a vast number of entrepreneurs, they have saved up a substantial amount to invest into their business venture. Some people believe that this is the only way you can build a successful business, skipping the belief that time is the same, and a valuable commodity.

To conclude how much financial wealth you have, you don't need to look at your bank account, instead, we're going to relate it back to time. Think about the dollar amount per hour you'd work for, just to make money. This could be $10, $15, or even $20+. Whatever figure you come up with will help you ascertain how cash-rich you are.

Another step is working out opportunity cost, and this is a figure in dollars which you're giving up to work in someone else's business. For every minute you work for someone else, you're sacrificing a minute working on your business, so, you are principally selling your time for financial gain.

The more money you say you'd work for an hour, the more money-rich you'd be. The less money you'd work for, per hour, the more time-rich you'd be.

Finding the Balance

Once you've worked out the time and money you have, you'll then need to find the best balance. It's a fact, the more time wealth you possess, the more time you'll need to work on your business, and if you don't have a substantial amount of time, you can't buy it back with the money you earn, by selling your time.

The good thing is, when you have an Amazon business, you're able to create plenty of both. The key is to launch systems which allow you to determine the hours you work, while still reaping the rewards from the time you invested into your business in the beginning.

Once you find the balance between time-rich and money-rich, you can determine which systems will help to scale your business. Even if you don't have a great deal of money, you'll find there's additional time in your life which you can now use to build those systems and generate more money.

This is your goal; you'll want to aim for it with your Amazon business, and by applying your two key resources, you're able to grow your business much quicker than if you had little of either of these.

33

Outsourcing Business

CHAPTER 33

You need to ask yourself, what is the ultimate dream for your Amazon business? Is it to increase cash in your pocket? Or, is it to leave full-time employment and start your own company? Maybe it's to replace regular, routine work, completely, all while earning an income which allows you to follow your passion. Only you know these answers.

A great number of people are oblivious to the fact that this is truly possible, and there's even more who believe that if something's too good to be true, then it usually is.

If you don't put the work in early on, or create systems to help achieve this, then perhaps this would be the case, but, you can assure yourself that it is possible. And, in building a business which will allow you to earn a passive income. It has to be true; there are vast numbers of entrepreneurs who've done exactly this.

This is the main goal for lots of people who've started their own business, and with the economy being how it is today, it is very possible and achievable.

Over the years, entrepreneurs have started businesses and sacrificed a significant amount of their time, only to find they are unable to buy this time back.

They might go on for years slugging away with their projects, only to discover that they fall short when the time comes, and that they are reaching their golden years. Setting up any business like this is slightly different from just running through the actions. Actually, it's all about you creating systems and installing procedures which allow your business to run by itself, and independently of you, regardless of the amount of time and effort you put in.

Where Can You Start?

If you find yourself at a loss of where you should start in regard to taking a step back and letting the business run without you, you should ask yourself one question: "What do I hate doing the most?"

An Amazon business isn't always plain sailing and, in fact, there are times when you'll feel like calling it a day and giving up altogether, and it is at these times which you'll quickly find out the answer to that question of what you hate doing the most...

There's many people who struggle in answering that question, and that's okay, it can be a normal reaction as there's a stigma around hating your work. But knowing it can help it to *not become* somewhat toxic. Hate could be seen as being too strong a word, but there are specific things which you find you can do effortlessly, and focusing on these makes sense.

Every one of us has one thing in business which we would rather not do because we aren't good at, or because it takes us too much time. The results we achieve don't add much value to the business. This feeling does have its value because it's a good indicator of where you'll begin creating systems, right up to outsourcing these tasks from "your already" busy schedule.

When you remove this task from your to-do list, it'll provide more time to spend doing jobs you do enjoy doing, and it'll give you a significant energy and motivation boost. This is mostly because you remove the draining resistance throughout your day.

Many people think this is taking an easy route, and they don't want to feel lazy or avoid doing what they should. This is entirely the wrong way to go about it. Running a business is much different, actually.

How to Establish Your FBA System

CHAPTER 34

Every successful entrepreneur understands their business must be a separate entity from them, and this is what makes the difference between entrepreneurs and small business owners, when compared to self-employed people. The theory is: buying back your time, and spending it in other ways. This could be building your career, spending time with family, or enjoying your time and money with life's little luxuries.

Here, we'll cover establishing the first system for your Amazon business. It is straightforward and simple, and while it might only save you five minutes here or there, as your business grows, the aggregate of time you save can surge, exponentially. When you create this system you'll have the inspiration to develop more for other tasks you perform yourself.

Don't Type Twice

You can see if you're heading in the right direction by using the "don't type twice" rule, where it says you shouldn't do the same task twice, especially if no value is added.

Now, you can start establishing systems to ensure that your time is spent wisely, and that anything you do, only needs to be done once. Then, the system takes care of the rest. A good example being: emails, and although they are an essential part of any business on a daily basis, once you sell product on Amazon, you'll be receiving countless customer emails each day. Here you must be sure customer service is efficient and effective. The standard of your customer service can affect the chance of getting good reviews.

The downside being; most emails will be similar (or the same), and you'll have customers asking very similar questions about the same products, which will become exhausting. Fortunately, your first system can help. You will find your messages in about 10 to 15 categories, and you need to avoid sending the same answers each time.

These replies don't add any value to your business and they aren't the best use of your time. When you send emails on a topic you know will arise again, it's time to create an email template. This could be about refunds, delivery time, and explanation of features, or just help with a problem that's always asked about.

From this point, you should start saving emails you send out with the name of the template, and this could be for "Product Refund" or "Feature Description," etc.

This is straightforward, and you'll only need to change a few keywords when adapting the email to a customer's specific inquiry. The first thing you need to add (which is specific) is the customer's name, and then other details which are unique. Once you've done this, save the email as a template and add a few tags.

How to Add Tags

When you add tags, you're supporting yourself for the future when you've got quite a few templates, and need to locate one. These tags need to include the subject line, product name, solution, and anything else which you think matches the situation.

This helps save lots of time when you search through old emails. It might not sound like it will save a lot of time, but as business grows, you'll have a huge influx of emails, and so time savings will be considerable in this regard.

Also, once you've hired a virtual assistant, you'll quickly find that this will help their work also, as they will be able to quickly locate a template based on the tags which match the situation that is being dealt with at the time.

Product Reviews and Multiplying Them

CHAPTER 35

Plenty of product reviews are crucial to the success of any product you sell on Amazon. You'll notice products which sit at the top of search results; they nearly-always have the most product reviews.

Every Amazon seller must do all they can in encouraging customers to write reviews. Waiting for a customer's response can take forever. When you first launch your product, these reviews are indispensable for increasing the rankings.

You must be proactive with customers when asking for reviews, because waiting for them can cost you thousands in lost sales. In many cases, the person who leaves a review of their own accord is an unhappy customer.

When you ask customers to leave a review, they'll leave more honest answers on how they feel, and whether their experience was good or bad.

This section also connects to the earlier part of sending emails from templates, and in making sure your customer service doesn't falter.

Templates for Reviews

As we saw earlier, we showed the idea of creating a template for customer service queries. Here, we'll also look at the concept of another template for customers to use and leave a review.

These review templates are another element when creating systems to run your business, and they are as important as providing excellent customer service. Actually, they are a driving force for sales and keeping rankings high, and in keeping satisfied customers "happy."

There are tools you can use to hopefully get customers to leave a review. The first being Feedback Genius, and you should take a look because it's one of the most powerful tools available. This tool allows you create templates to send out automatically, at programmed times. This is very useful as it saves the effort of writing a message to send to your customer.

What you should experience from this is; a raft of reviews, even if sale volumes remain the same. This is the premier advantage of auto-responding emails which allow you to communicate with customers, without manually creating these emails, each and every time. Customers feel like they're being treated better because they are receiving emails which are personalized.

The reason is: Amazon often feels impersonal. Your brand, conversely, is different, and you can send automated emails which have the personal touch, even if it is to only check that they received their product.

Setting up Templates

The first steps toward forming a system and requesting reviews from your customers are the creation of templates for each product. It might also be worth creating individual templates for both your current customers and new customers, who might feel special if they're returning for a second purchase.

Actually, the more personal your templates, the better the experience for your customers, which means your chance of receiving positive reviews from them is more likely, too. Not all emails need to be personalized, however, the more which are; the better. But you should keep it simple.

The goal in doing this is to save yourself time, and not do more work, and when you use an automatic email app along with writing personalized templates, you'll see a significant increase in the number of reviews you can receive.

The Beauty and Power of Good Reviews

The more reviews that you can generate and receive for your product, the higher you should see your conversion rate becoming. The reason being is that customers are drawn to products when they look at a large number of reviews.

You will soon find generating reviews has a compounding effect, and when you start sending out emails to paying customers, they'll begin to provide more reviews. The impact of this being that your rankings can rise, which should, in turn, lead to more sales.

With these increased sales you'll have more customers leaving reviews, and the spiral increases, further upward. It can happen quickly, and when you use a tool such as Feedback Genius, you should notice an improvement in positive results.

The app does have a cost, but for any business, it should be a small price to pay, especially when the return on your investment is boundless. The software does have a free trial, so you can test its capabilities before deciding whether or not to hand over any money.

Outsourcing Profit Tracking and Other Essentials

CHAPTER 36

Once you find the elements you like, and the ones that take all your time in your Amazon business, the next step is in understanding which add value to the company, and which tasks are best left to your automated or outsourced systems. One noteworthy part of your business which can take an enormous amount of time (without adding value) is profit tracking.

Profit tracking is where you go through each product and find the profit each time you place orders, and to do this, you need to look at the costs involved when selling a single unit. This includes everything from a PPC campaign to any costs of the systems that were created earlier. All these are added to your supplier cost price.

This is crucial to successfully running any business, but once you've done it once, each subsequent time will be a repetition of the same task. There are many tasks like this, and you might prefer to continue doing these because these are what you enjoy. As long as you follow through with the priorities of your business growth, because if these become stagnant, then you might be wise to outsource other areas of your business.

Recording Inventory

Inventory monitoring can be made more accessible by some tools you can use, and these can help with tracking your profits and sales. In this guide, we'll take a look at **SELLICS**.

The main module of SELLICS is its portal, and here you're presented with a range of tools and services, with the primary one being the inventory module.

When using this tool, you can enter the lead time for your product, and monitor your stock levels. Here it will alert you when you need to reorder. This can be a powerful tool which becomes more helpful when you're reaching more advanced stages of your business, and you have multiple products which require monitoring.

Once you have five or more products, you'll find inventory control quickly becomes overwhelming, especially with all the other tasks you still need to accomplish.

This can be highly stressful when there are significant changes in your business: such as your advertising campaigns, or adding new products or searching for new suppliers. This is the time to use tools which can work in the background, rather than you checking every day.

Tracking Your Profit

This is simple and straightforward with your first product, and once you start bringing in sales, it doesn't take too much effort to use a spreadsheet. This can give a quick view of your profit while your rankings climb.

Once your business starts to grow, and you begin to reinvest income into advertising, you might find that your spreadsheet gets harder to manage, and on some days, you might forget to list the figures you need to enter.

Once you begin adding further products, the entire job becomes cumbersome. Aside from this, values will change from Amazon for storage charges, etc. This occurs because stock rises and falls, so these changes affect profit margins across the board. Attempting to do this on a spreadsheet is nigh on impossible.

This tool allows you to track expenses, and everything from your advertising, including Amazon FBA fees, supplier costs, and your sales figures, for you to come up with your final number. This is clear and shows how much profit (or loss) you're making.

Calculations in Rankings

As this tool is a one-stop-shop for Amazon sellers, you can use this tool to calculate where your rankings sit for particular keywords. You now know how essential rankings are, and that they are a key component in deciding whether products are successful.

This is particularly useful when launching new products, and if you want to gain traction (fast) in the first few weeks. Instead of leaving everything up to trial and error, the use of SELLICS can analyze keywords and give a day-to-day report on performance.

Are these Tools of Use?

Even though there are plenty of tools available, you still need to decide if they are going to help take your business in the right direction. Every Amazon seller is different, and many prefer doing things (such as their profit tracking and inventory control) personally. Freedom of time is a goal many people seek, but that's not to say it is for everyone.

A lot of these tasks you're capable of doing yourself, and it's your choice if you decide the time spent on this work is more valuable than if you trade it for more free time. You could save 25 to 30 hours every month by automating these tasks, depending on what stage you're at with your business and its income.

37

Automated Product Sourcing

CHAPTER 37

Now that we've covered customer communications, outsourcing profit tracking, keyword research, and inventory reporting, you can move to the next step and fully automate your Amazon business.

If you are introverted and have a dislike of face-to-face dealings with other people, then the next step is your product sourcing and supplier communications. Many people struggle in this area, and find it quite draining if you're new to business environments.

The challenge is that: your business needs to grow, and you've no choice but to continue sourcing new products, placing recurring orders, and negotiating with suppliers.

Automated Specialized Services

We have mentioned a couple of time a service called Guided

Imports, and this company takes care of a negotiation process via a specialized team who's highly skilled in this task. They come with training in Chinese culture and also have regular suppliers on their books. Therefore, they already have stable working relationships with suppliers you might already be contacting.

When you have a team such as this at your disposal, it can allow you to step back from the negotiation process. Negotiation takes years to master, and this shows the size of discounts seller s can achieve. With high volumes of purchases, a service like this can (all but) pay for itself.

Teams like this can also do much more than negotiations and they can make a request for new product samples too. Additionally, they'll also work with your suppliers to deliver designs, based on your instructions.

A service of this nature can take a fair chunk out of your budget and should be considered carefully. It is more advantageous if you have larger (rather than smaller) shipments, so you would need to decide whether it's right for you.

Top-Rated Customer Service

CHAPTER 38

One area where you can provide a premium aspect without spending any money is within the level of your customer service, and this has no concern about the size of your business.

First class customer service tells customers plenty about your business, and you will be faced with your fair share of customer inquiries which ranges from refunds, returns, and complaints, plus anything else which relates to your product.

Customer service is seen as one critical area of any business because it sets the perception of how customers see a company, and possessing a positive image helps enterprises to flourish.

When you have first-class customer service, they will keep returning, and they start to feel a personal affinity for your brand. This might help maintain five-star reviews, which should help to increase sales, as well.

This task can be time-consuming, and it's not a natural thing to do for many people, because not everyone is a "people" person. With this in mind, they might feel too much pressure in making customers happy, and at this point, you can unlock the secret which could help your business immeasurably, and give you a chance to focus on what you feel is most important. This secret is that of virtual assistants. We'll cover these now.

Virtual Assistants

Virtual assistants can be located in any country around the world. All of their work would be completed over the internet. This gives you access to a vast resource pool from which you can choose, and enables you to be more flexible in the hiring process.

Virtual assistants can specialize in various tasks. Some help with basic administration tasks, while others are skilled and can handle some of the more in-depth tasks. The ones which you prefer to outsource.

So, we are looking at virtual assistants who specialize in customer service practices, and often come with proven track records in this field. This can add a wealth of value to any business, and provides customers with a top-rated experience when making contact regarding their concerns.

During the early stages of your business, it isn't crucial to look at this level of outsourcing, but when you start building up reviews and start thinking of adding a second and a third product, the hiring of a VA can give you the time you need for these products to be introduced.

Finding Virtual Assistants

A good number of people wouldn't know where to begin looking for virtual assistants, and it can be crucial to making sure you get the best one. And because they work on the internet, that's where you'll find them.

There are numerous websites which allow you to post your position, and from there you'll receive many applications. Prices will vary due to VA location, and also for how many hours you wish them to work each day. A VA might be economical, but they don't work for free and so still need to be respected as an employee.

The best marketplace is a site called Upwork.com. This is the number one site on the planet, so if they don't have the person you're looking for, then you'll struggle in any other freelance marketplace.

This site matches freelancers with businesses, and VAs are one of the most represented groups. The site offers plenty of flexible options which allow you to tailor your job posting to fit your needs. You can hire a virtual assistant full time, part time, or even on an ad-hoc basis.

To create an account on Upwork is free, and this will allow you to see what freelancers are currently available.

Virtual Assistant Job Posting

When you come to create your job posting, it will help to be specific about the job details. You can create a template, although some are offered by Upwork too.

As things change rapidly online, and Upwork is no different, the design of templates can change quickly, and as there is a massive resource pool, the freelancers obviously look for the best jobs.

It is far better to be clear and concise and use bullet points to lay out duties. This way, there is no confusion on what you expect from the VA.

Deciding on the Right Virtual Assistant

There are criterion you should look for when trying to find the best freelancer for the job, and it should be seen as any regular interview. You need to ask what their skills are and what software you want them to use.

It doesn't matter what you ask, there will be more applicants than you know what to do with. Some will need to be discarded, and this type you can see from the quality of their application.

A good many also copy and paste their applications, and then change a minor part. These are the ones who you should look at "weeding out" because they answer to every job posted. The essential criterion is attention to detail and organization, and this is regardless of any task which they are performing.

When you're first starting, it's best to hire someone who's done it all before, compared to someone you need to guide through the process.

With Upwork, you can easily employ your freelancer for a test period of a week or two, and pay them accordingly. This can help you to get a feel for them, and check you can both work together well. Remember, that once your trial is over you will be requested to give feedback for your VA.

Your First Virtual Assistant System

Now you have your virtual assistant, your operations should feel like you've doubled your work capacity. This will, of course, depend on tasks you've given to them.

You need to be sure that you provide your VA with plenty of work to keep them occupied, while you focus on time freedom, or concentrate on expanding your business.

As was mentioned, you can get them emailing customers manually or maintaining an automatic email responder. This might take a significant amount of time, but when they are experienced, they should be able to complete it quickly. After this, you can ask them to take care of inventory level monitoring, profit tracking, and keyword research.

After this, you can give them the task of tracking seller feedback and the removal of negative seller feedback. Other tasks can include asking your VA to chase customers, and asking them to turn positive seller feedback into a positive review.

A good VA can take over any part of your business you would like to remove from your task list, and as your business grows, you might like to hire another VA and have your entire operation running by itself.

Advanced Systems

When a VA has taken over a lot of your work, you can start building more advanced systems. This would be known as a "standard operating procedure" and will involve describing any functions you'd like any virtual assistant to complete (in a video). And here, their task would be to transcribe the video, and from there, they're able to create their task list by using the transcription.

This allows instructions to be given without adding complications or confusions. This is essential for creating a broader sense of time-freedom in your business.

Find Complimentary Items for Your Amazon Products

CHAPTER 39

When you to decide on your next product (and it will be running alongside your first), there are several methods you can use to be sure the product you choose will also become a success.

One way of doing this is by looking at your customers' "reviews" and "wish lists." This is helpful because you can see what they've purchased and what they are planning to buy in the future.

Customer Profiles

When you look at a customer's wish list, you will see their purchasing habits. As an example, if you see they are purchasing kitchen equipment after buying one of your products, there's a good chance their next purchase will also be something for their kitchen.

It might be the case they've moved into a new house or are renovating their kitchen, and so would like similar items to match. Another method is by looking at what they've reviewed, and you'll spot various things, and each one will give you more insight into the customer that's purchased items of yours.

Knowing Your Customer

You will see similar potential customers in your surroundings. As an example, if you are marketing something related to the gym, consider asking around and it won't be long before someone who goes to the gym says that a particular item is hugely popular.

This gives you the idea of what they are likely to buy next. This can be more difficult, but it has the advantage of a more in-depth exploration geared toward the kind of customers you sell to.

Suggestions from Amazon

One more area where you can look is: Amazon's powerful algorithm. You can look at the *recently bought* and *related products* of what is trending. This gives ideas of what is being bought together, and what the uptrend is.

The advantage of this method is: that instead of looking at individuals per say, you're referencing millions of customers and what their purchases are. And that, in itself, is priceless.

Other Sellers

Lastly, you can see what your competitors offer their customers within the same niche. In some ways, this can be a shortcut when performing research yourself, but you'll need to be careful, and keep in mind that the product might be reaching the end of a favored stint.

It is best to avoid anyone else's brand entirely, as having a similar range of products means too hefty a completion, in many cases. Additionally, this defeats having a unique brand and offering your unique selling position. As a result, you're only saturating the market more, and making it difficult for both you and your competitor/s.

You can though, gain useful information from your competitors, and into the next steps you need to take in growing your own brand.

Success with Amazon FBA

CHAPTER 40

By working with Amazon, it's possible to expand to a six or seven figure business, and in this final section, we'll discuss what you need to grow your business to a million dollars (and above) in revenue.

We'll explore a social media strategy, a method of creating brands people know and trust, and ideas which will provide your business with long-term success.

Zero to Hero and a 100k-1M Business Plan

Your success on Amazon has a compounding effect, and with every dollar you make (and product you launch), your business growth will increase exponentially while making it easy, each consecutive time.

The reason being; you'll work out the optimum ways of doing

things, the right strategies to use, and so your business will be streamlined.

One common mistake is product sniping, and where you take a product from a niche for your first product (for this example, let's say a mixing bowl). For your second, you see an opening for gym equipment and identify another niche such as this. While the products might be profitable, you're missing out on the progress you can create for your brand.

Customers won't be coming back to purchase new items because their interests might not have been met.

Creating a successful brand involves focusing on a core niche and avoiding stretching yourself too thinly. You'll want to serve the customers that have an interest in what you are offering, and steer away from trying to help a wider market with a bunch of random products. This makes it far more challenging to build a brand.

Building your brand means expanding outside of Amazon, because being only on Amazon limits you to a single stream of income. With other areas outside, you have Shopify, WordPress with a WooCommerce plug-in, and endless streams you can turn into possibilities.

Your customers will recognize you away from Amazon, and this will build more credibility, thus offering higher exposure.

Finally, your brand should stand for something, because this will set you apart from other businesses and brands which are not just Amazon-based, but across the internet further, as well. When you have a mission statement, it allows you to define what your business means to its customers, and the driving force behind your business.

The Calculations

Here we're going to use basic math and demonstrate how easy it is to create a million-dollar brand.

Let's look at an example using average figures, some days are higher, and some are lower:

Say you have 10 daily sales of $25 per product.

You are going to make $250 revenue, and over the length of the year, that's around $90000.

10 x $25 = $250 and $250 x 365 = $91250

Once you have the systems in place, you can then start launching additional products. It should be noted: the first takes the longest. Let's say you launch another three products.

Now again, on average you're making, let's say, $1000 a day.

40 x $25=$1000 and $1000 x 365 = $365000.

This is a hugely simplified example, but you can see it isn't as difficult as you first imagined.

Consider now, over time, your present products improve, and so you'll be gaining more reviews, and climbing up the rankings faster. Each new product you release will relate to customers who purchased your previous products, and you'll soon be able to increase your conversion rates.

You will be on the fast-track to a million, with a product line of fewer than 10 items.

Utilizing First Amazon Product to Increase Income

Before thinking about your second product to build your brand, consider your first product, which still has untapped value. Apart from the product, there are numerous variations you can make to your first listing, which continues adding value to your product, and generates extra income too. This is something many sellers neglect, and they leave their money doing nothing.

Take a look at variables involved with your product. Conversion rates, as an example. There are numerous ways this could be maximized, so rather than five out of a hundred purchasing your product, you could double it (and have 10).

There are many ways to do this and it takes trial and error. For example, you can change the sales copy of your product listing, and the images, or possibly the title. Now compare with the previous analytics and see the effect it has.

Once you've got your listing right, consider the product because there are many variations you can alter to appeal to a broader range of customers. This can be the size of the product, if it was apparel, and then the colors, patterns, etc.

Keep in mind, while you can change variations, there does come the point of experiencing diminishing returns. This is where adding extra variety to your product no longer becomes worthwhile. An unusual color (as an example) may not sell as well.

The Big Power of Social Media

Social media can help your business to grow and expand, especially as customers become accustomed to your brand. The potential of social media is realized when you build true fans of your brand. It doesn't take millions of people, because in today's e-commerce landscape, you only need a "small niche following" of fans and an excellent social media presence, just to help keep them engaged.

This is well-known as the "one thousand true fans theory." And if you've got one thousand true fans that are easily going to purchase any product you release, you're destined to make a decent living over an extended period of time.

With extraordinary customers that give lifetime value, you can hypothetically continue to expand your business by incremental changes which increase your profits over time.

As an example, if you have a product which sells for $10, and you've got 1000 potentials looking to purchase this product, you search for ways to increase the price by around 10% (or the volume attained by 10%). Now you can still make a significant profit increase, just by exploiting the power of your followers.

In Conclusion

Through this fully comprehensive title, I truly hope you've learned and gained the understanding about the secrets needed to succeed with Amazon FBA. And to founding and effectively growing an Amazon business, and a private label brand.

The information which has been handed to you is intended to help you to launch yourself into a niche market. Aside from this, you can set yourself at a distance from competitors by providing similar and better products.

This is a mighty triumph reaching this far in starting your own business, and you've likely met many difficulties along the way already, but it's the steps which you take from this point which become the driving force toward your success.

During the course of this title, you've discovered how to spot potential markets in need of improvement, and upgrades over what the other competitors may have on offer. You've learned how you validate ideas through various channels, as well as redesigning and recreating products to add a unique selling position.

From there; we dealt with negotiations and communications with your suppliers, including how to establish long-term, successful relationships. We then moved along with creating your first listing, and how you can go on and rise to the top of the Amazon search engine rankings, just by using your targeted keywords and having a compelling sales copy.

This was followed by creating glorious images to grab customer attention, and how best to utilize the many marketing avenues to acquire profitable advertising campaigns.

Towards the end, you were given some final words on how you should structure your business and build long lasting success, and not only in the Amazon marketplace, but also in creating a brand which your customers know and trust. This helps in allowing you to grow your business well into the future.

I thoroughly hope you've gained a lot from this big title. I'm sending all the luck to you in your Amazon FBA journey.

Yours sincerely, *James Moore.*

P.S. Always have belief in yourself; it's what sets you apart from everyone else. You have the ability to create anything you want... yes, I'm speaking directly to you! Good luck; go get 'em, they're waiting for you...

Printed in the USA
CPSIA information can be obtained
at www.ICGtesting.com
LVHW052027300724
786935LV00007B/187